THE COLOR ZOO

A TO Z

ANIMAL GUIDE

By: Darien Gulley

This book belongs to: ________________________

My favorite

animal is:

____

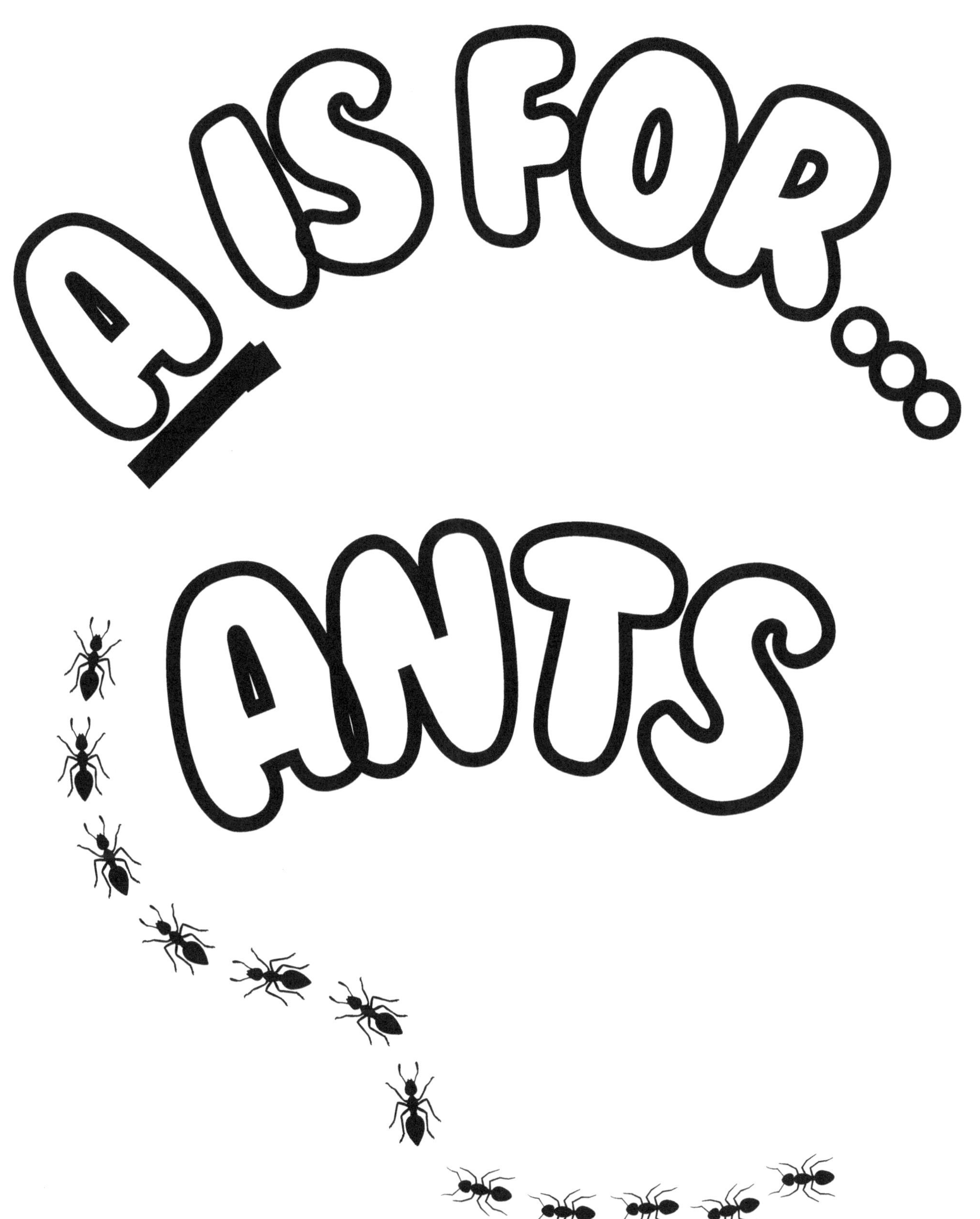
A IS FOR...
ANTS

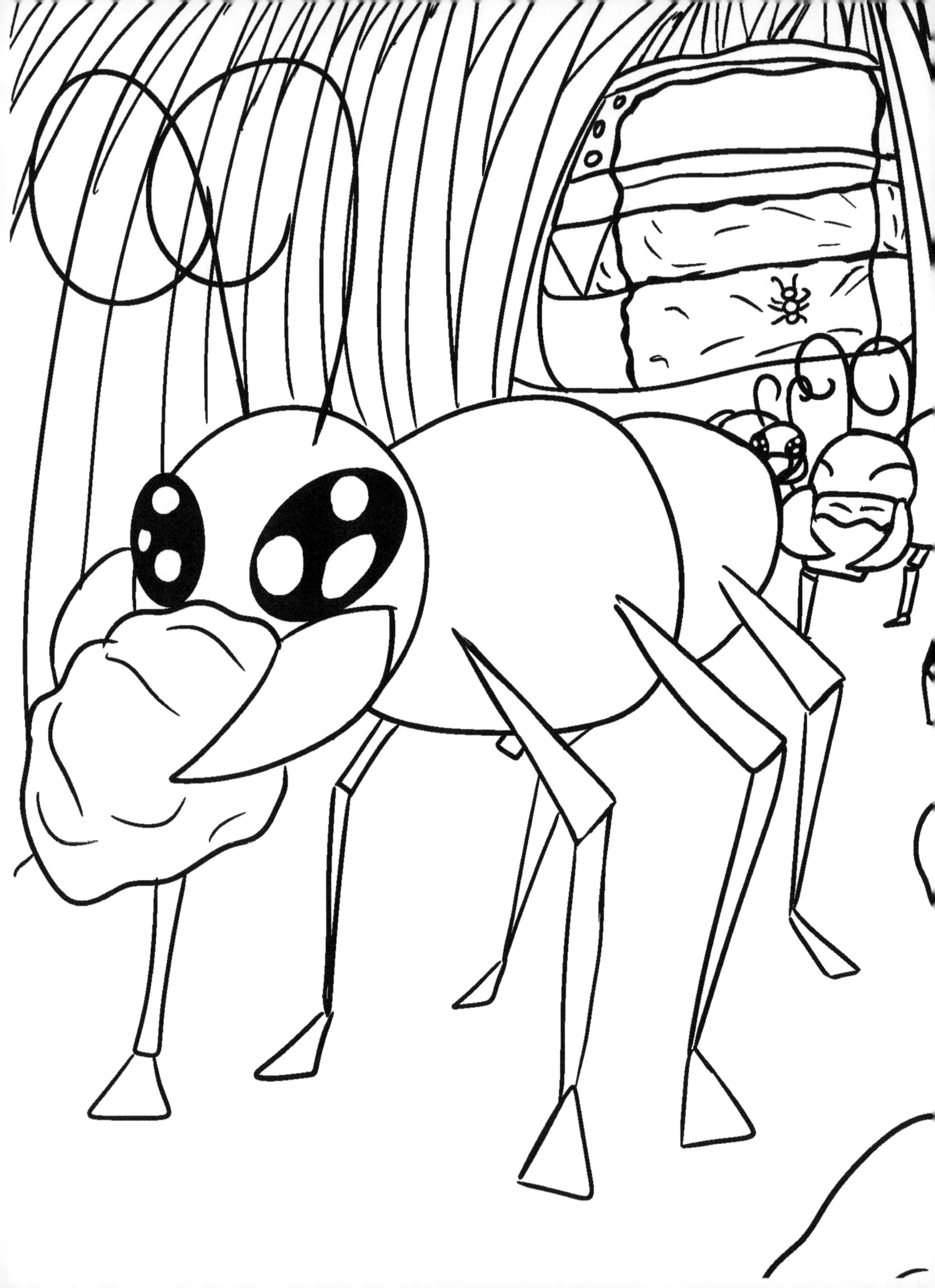

B IS FOR...

BEARS

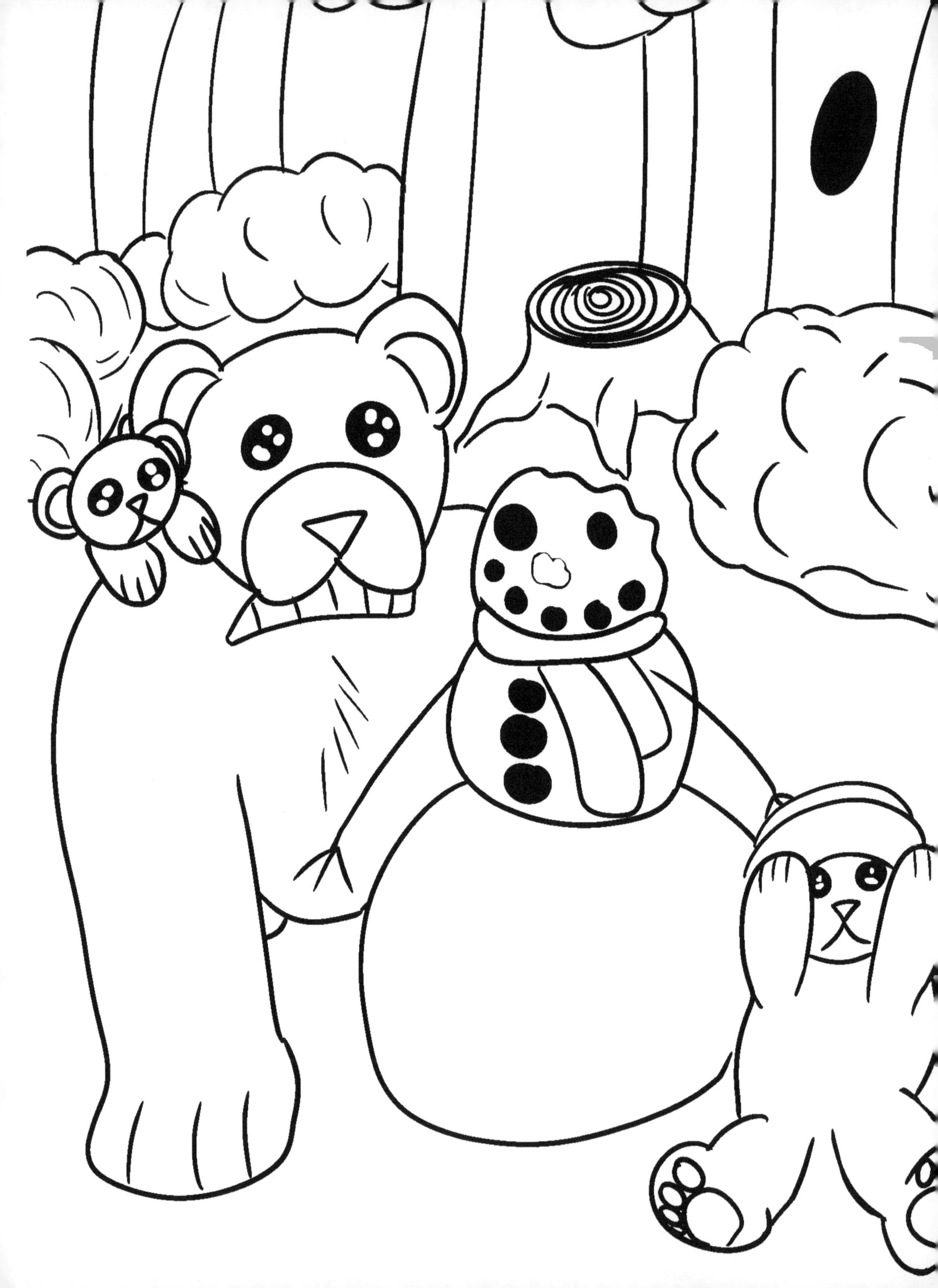

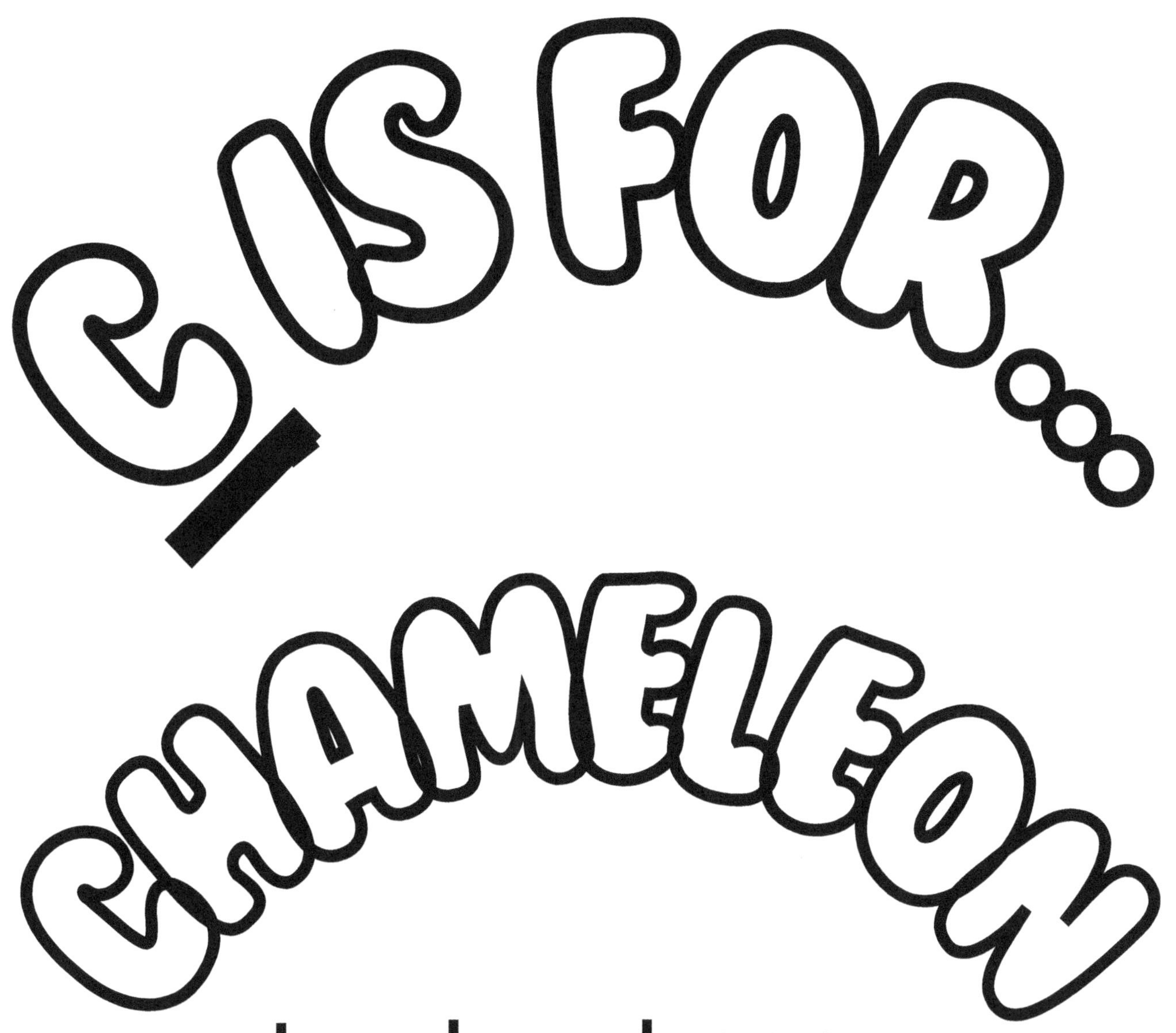

Is a chameleon a...

a. Mammal

b. Reptile

c. Fish

d. Amphibian

e. Bird

f. Bug

(Answers on last page)

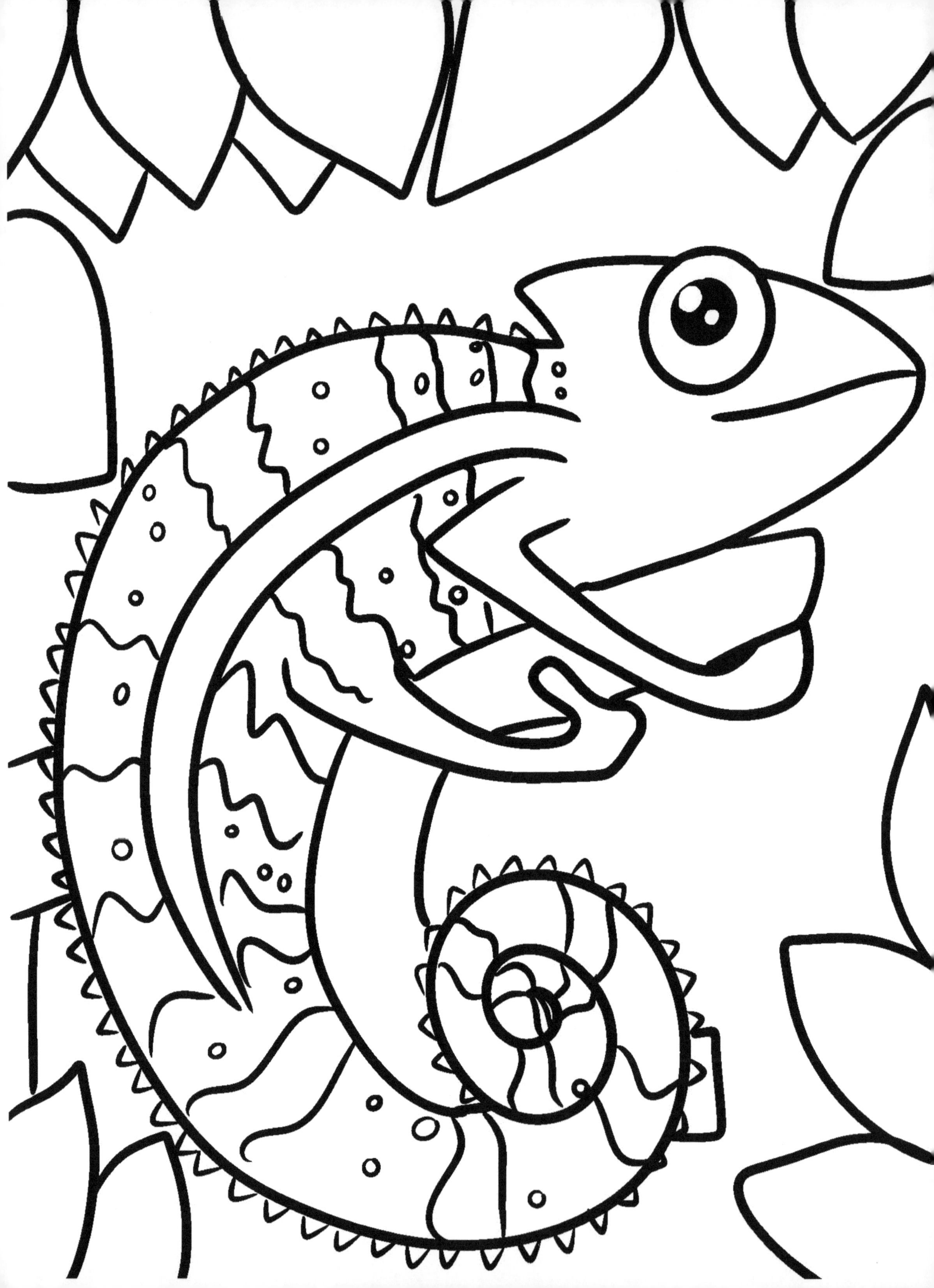

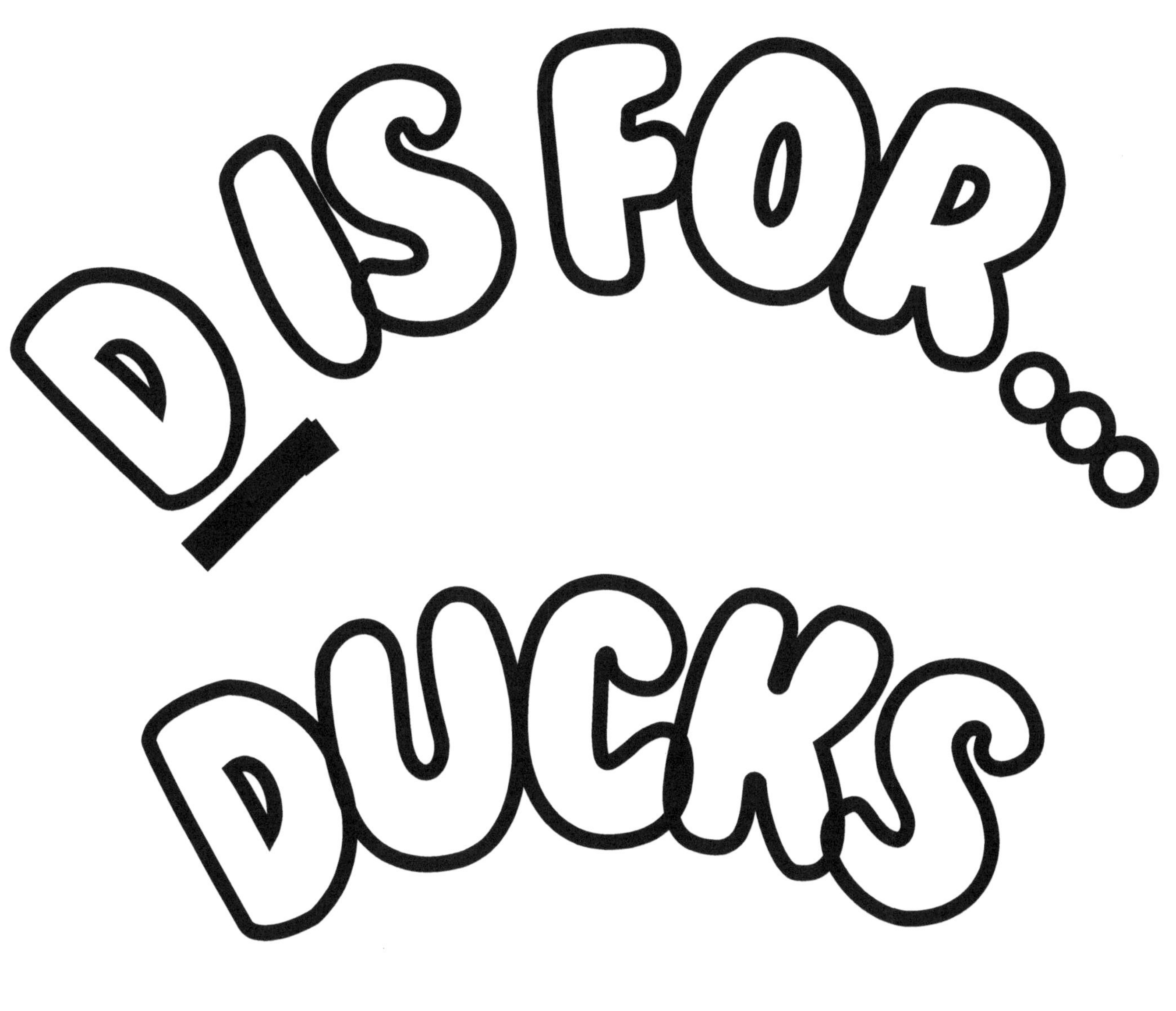

D IS FOR...
DUCKS

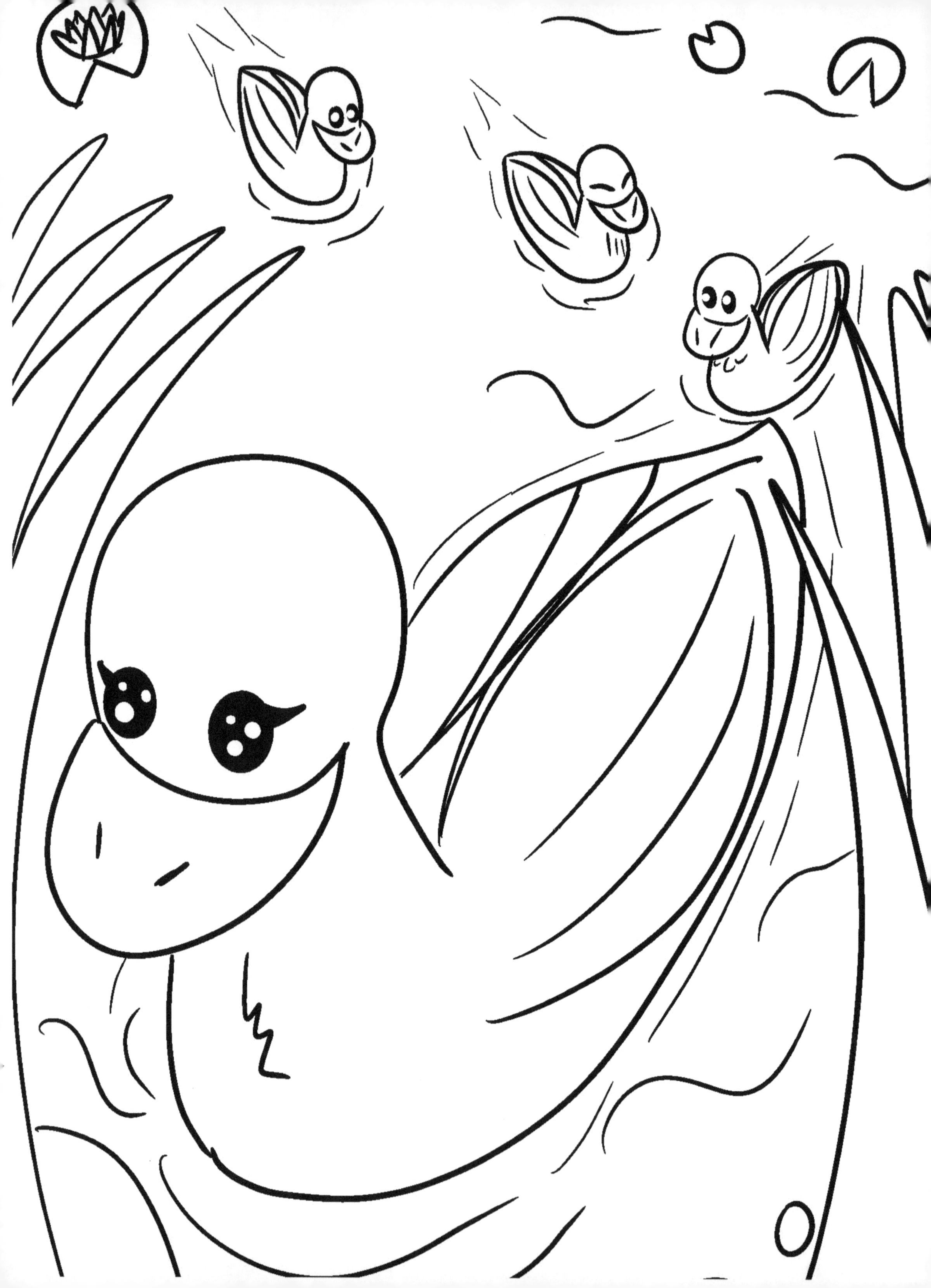

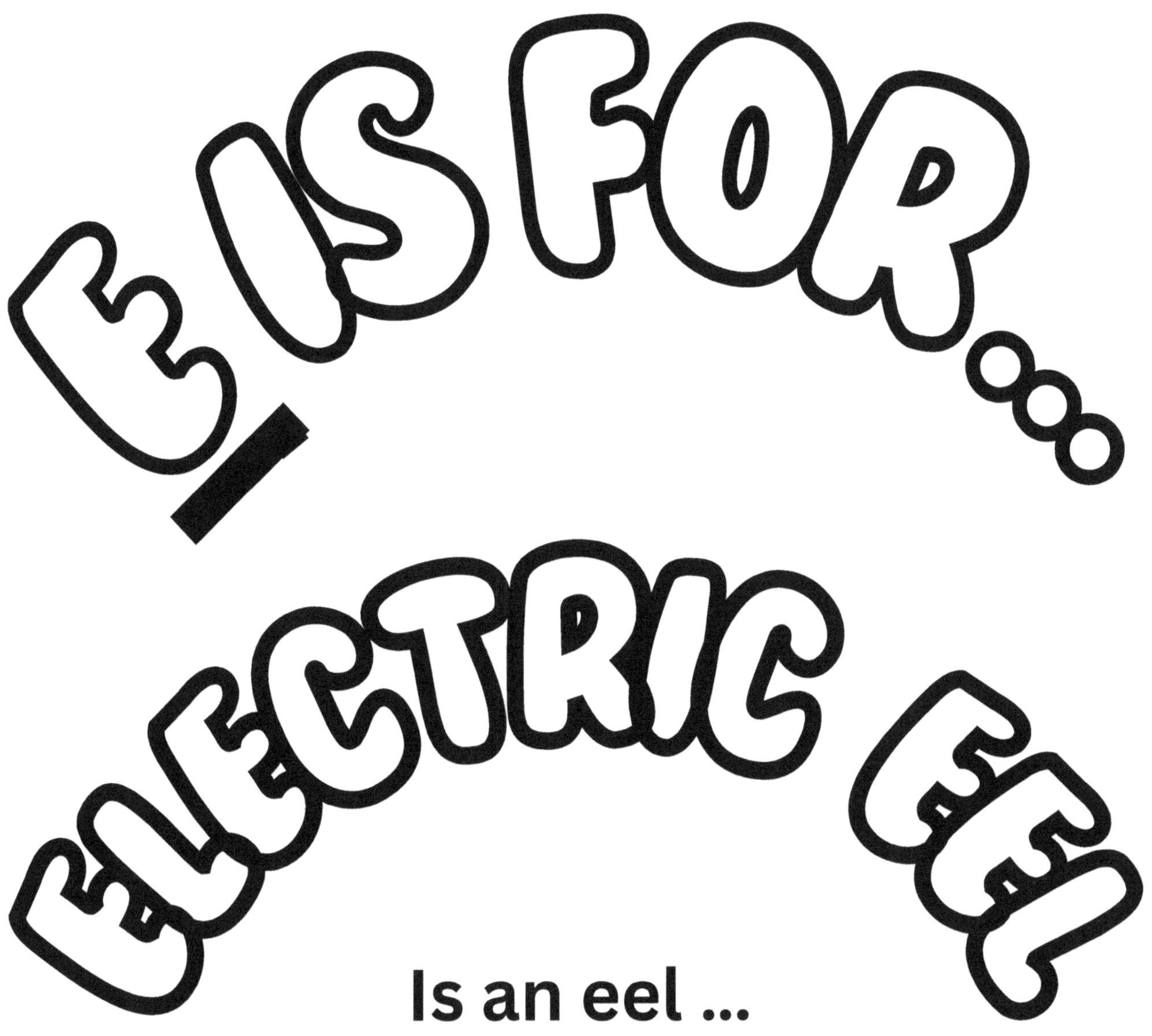

Is an eel ...

a. Cold Blooded
b. Warm Blooded
c. No Blooded

(Answers on last page)

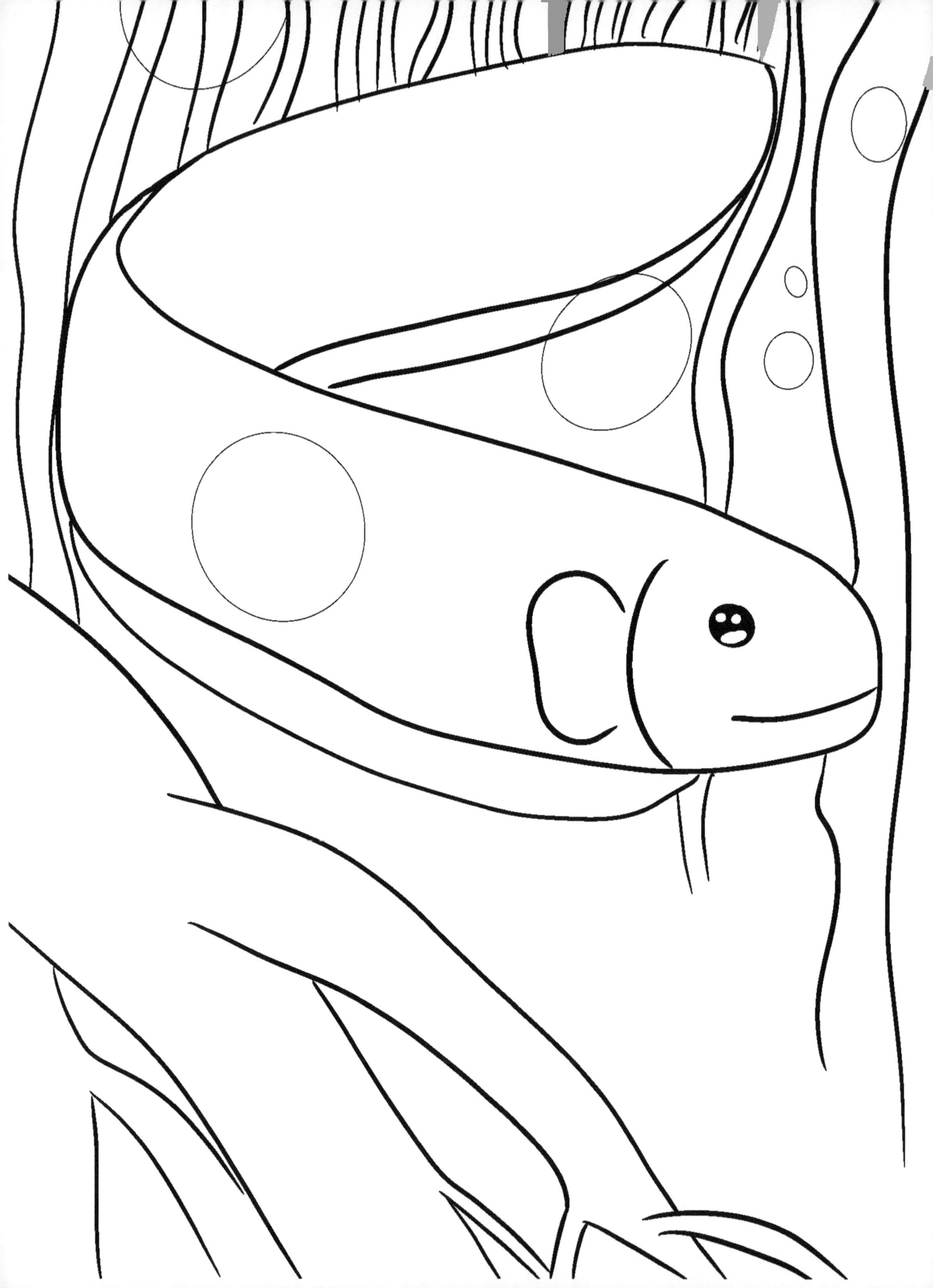

F IS FOR...

FROGS

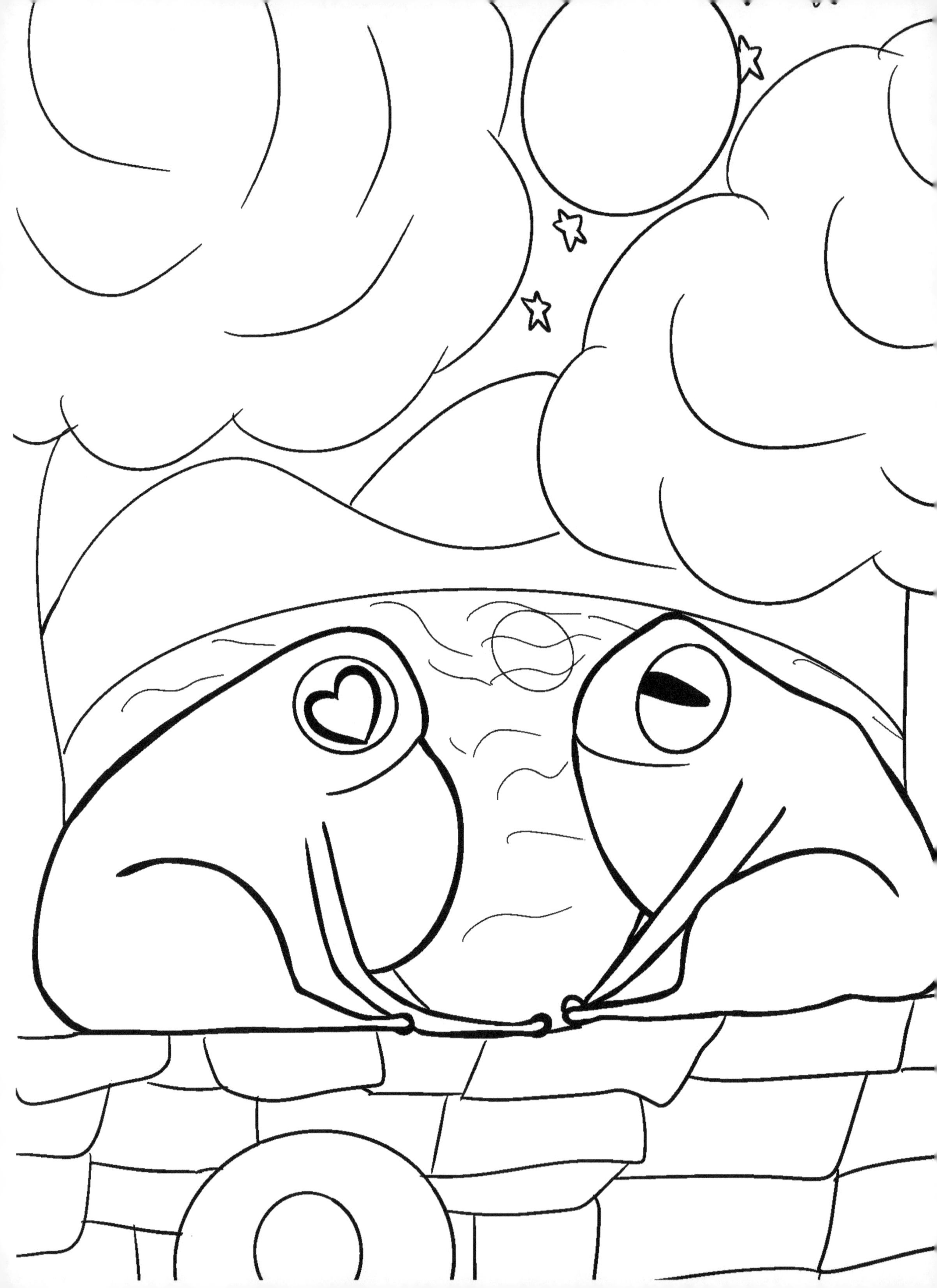

G IS FOR...

GECKO

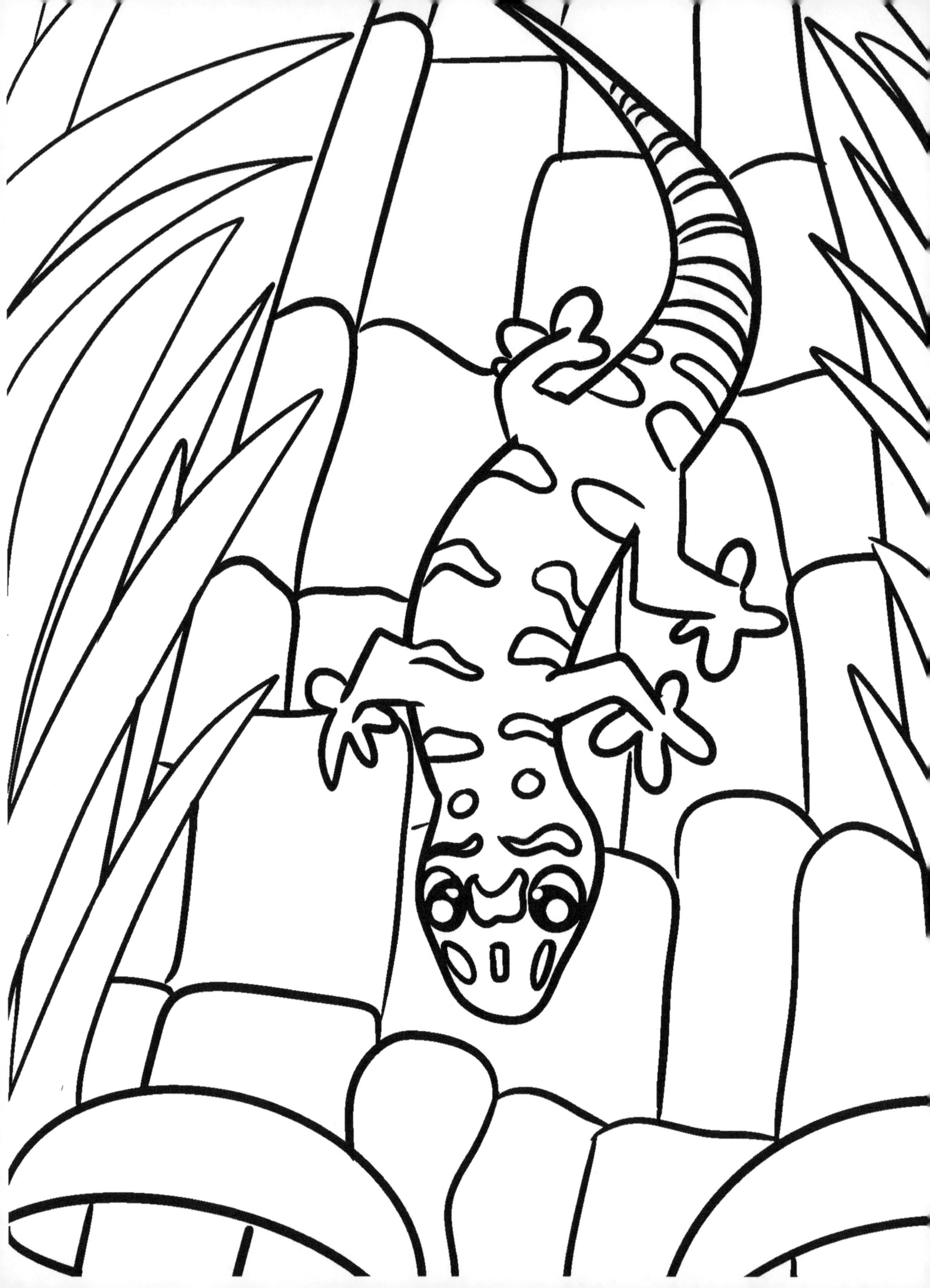

H IS FOR...

HUMMINGBIRDS

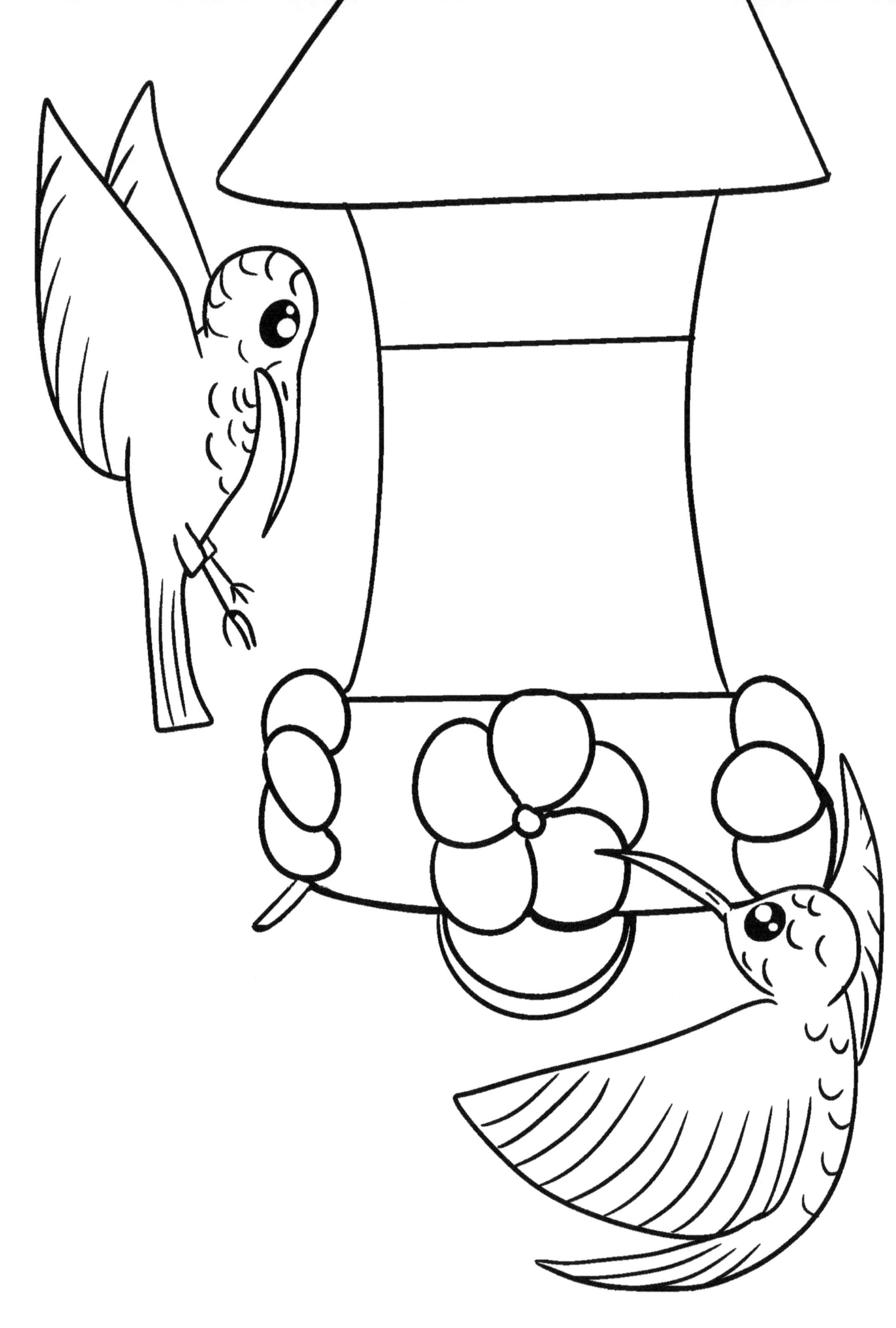

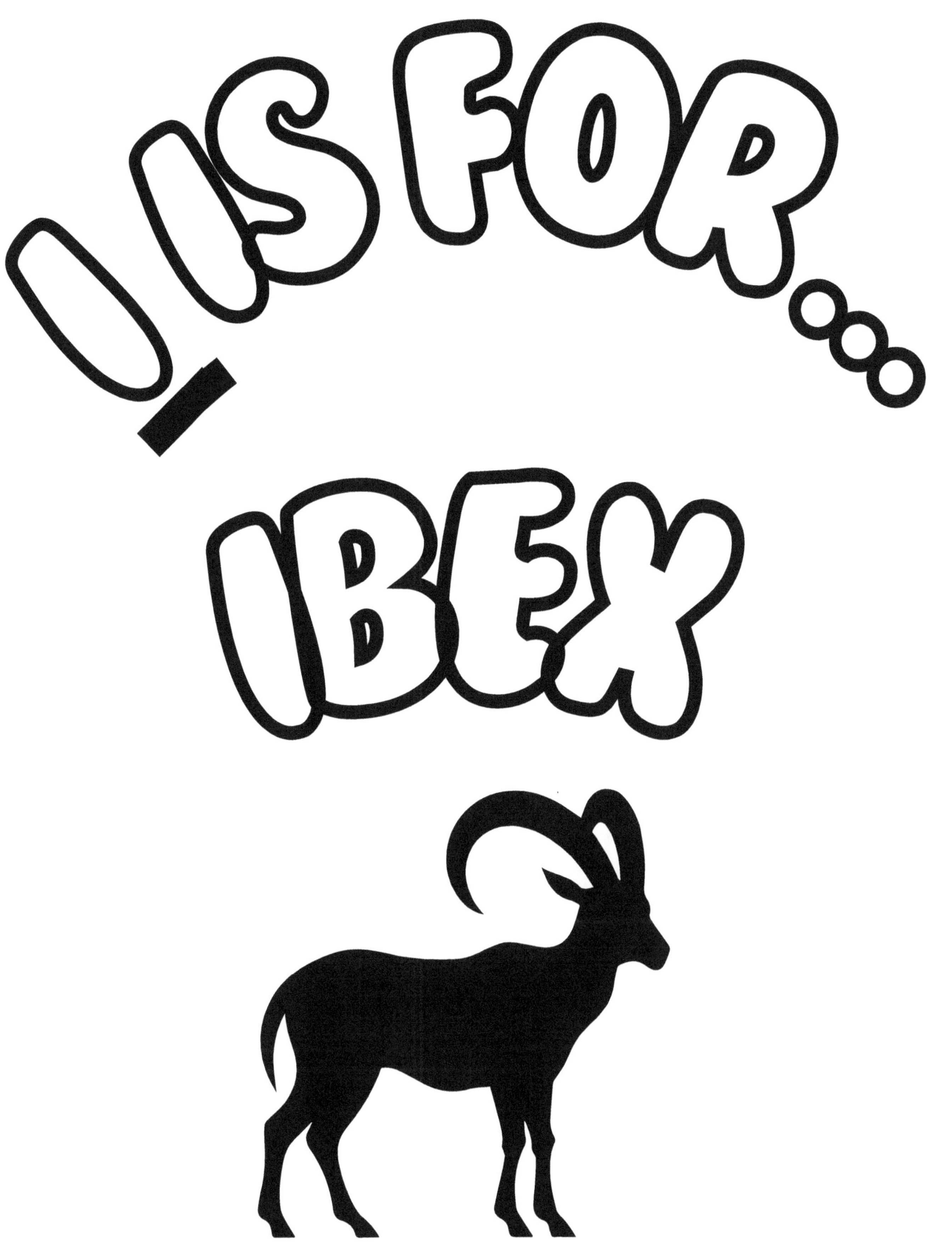
I IS FOR...
IBEX

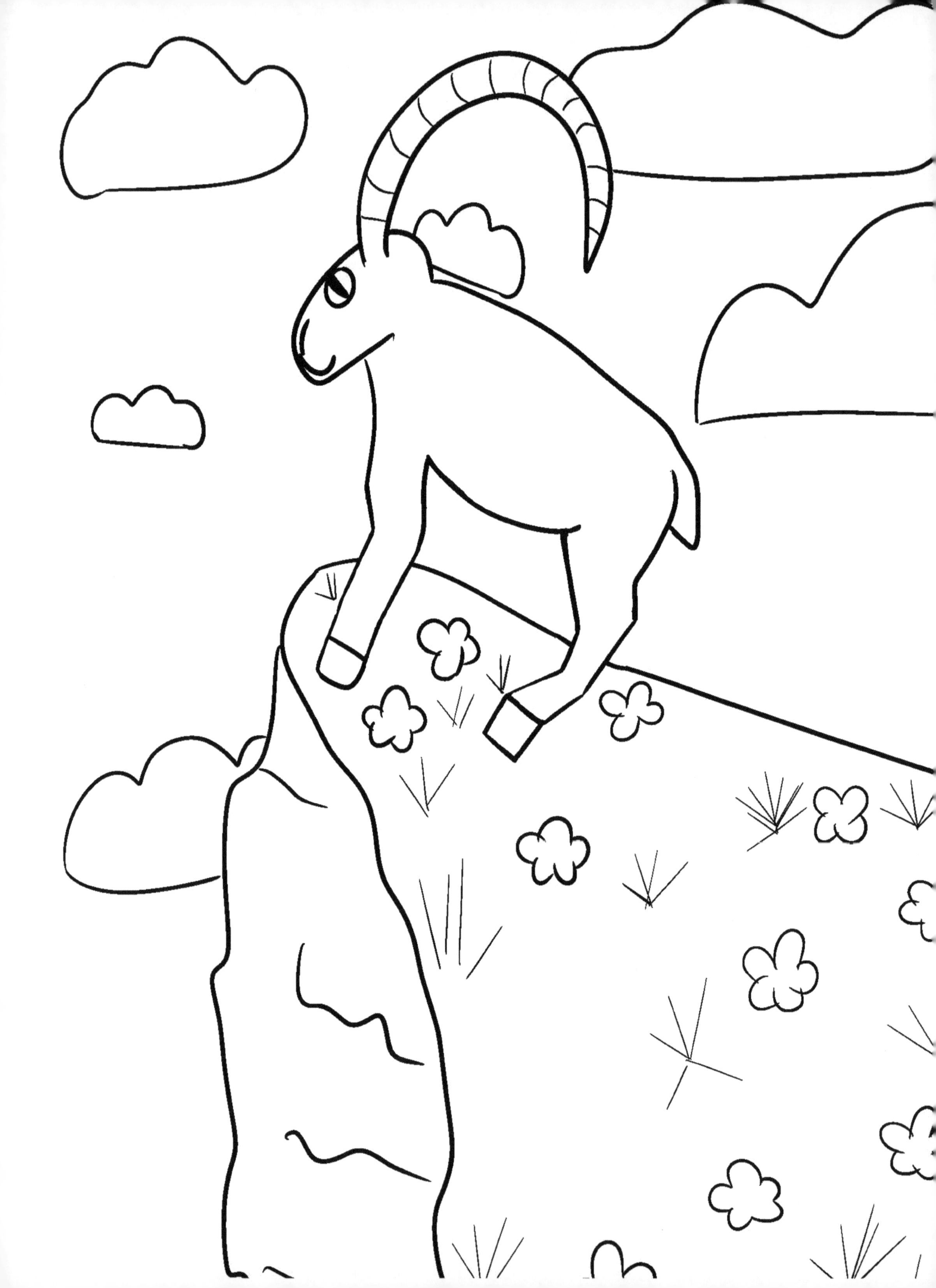

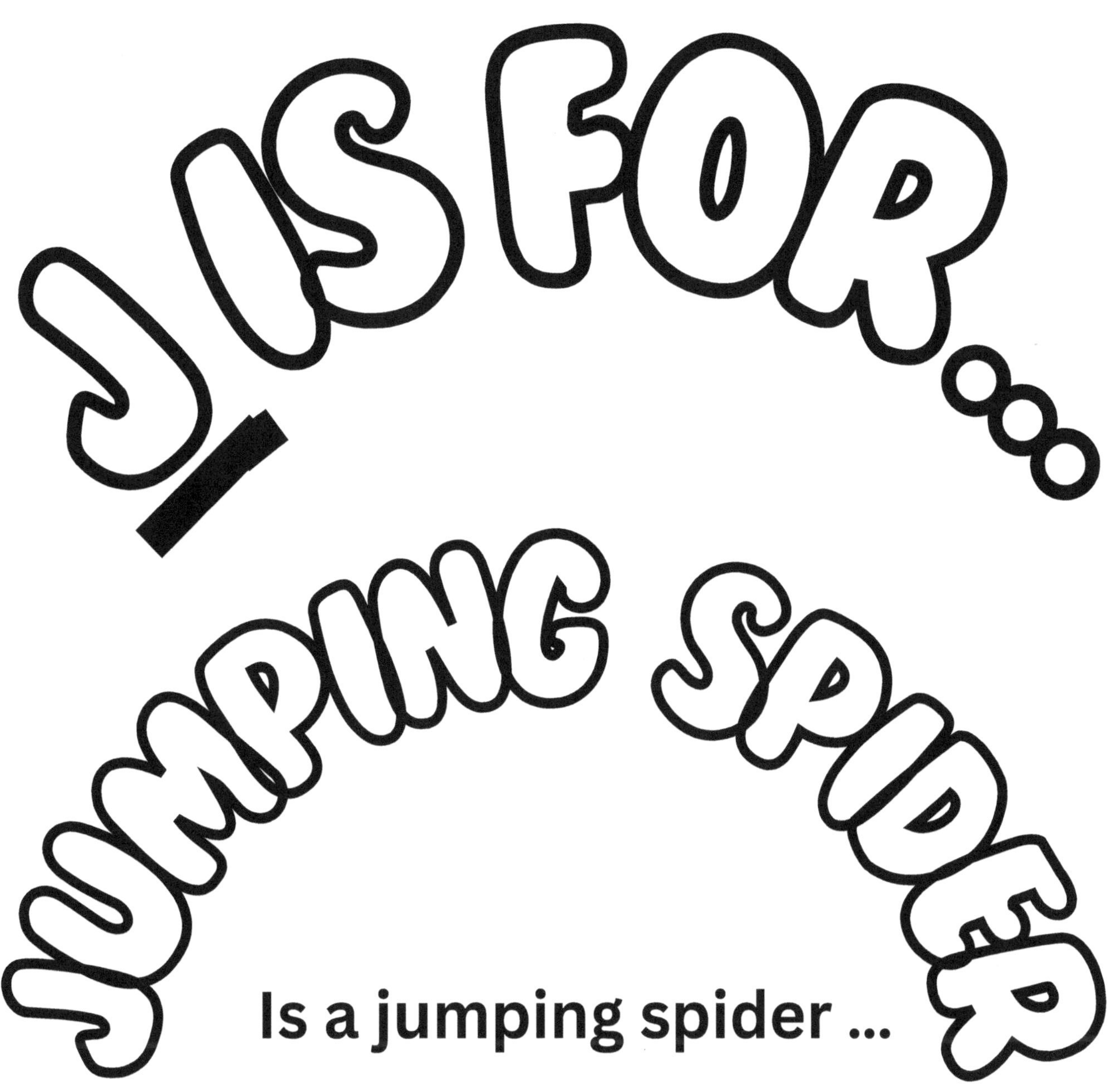

Is a jumping spider ...

a. Cold Blooded

b. Warm Blooded

c. No blooded

(Answers on last page)

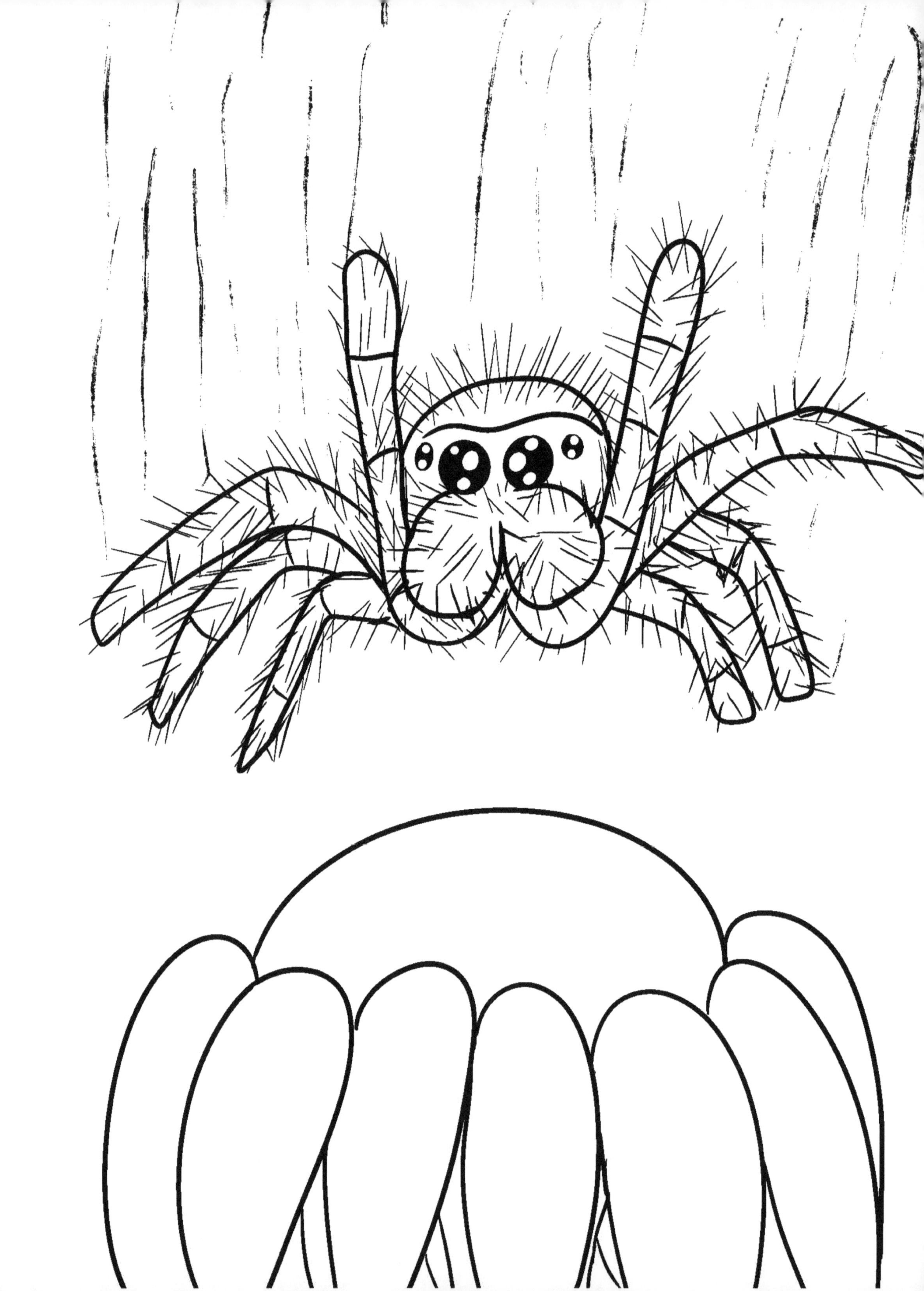

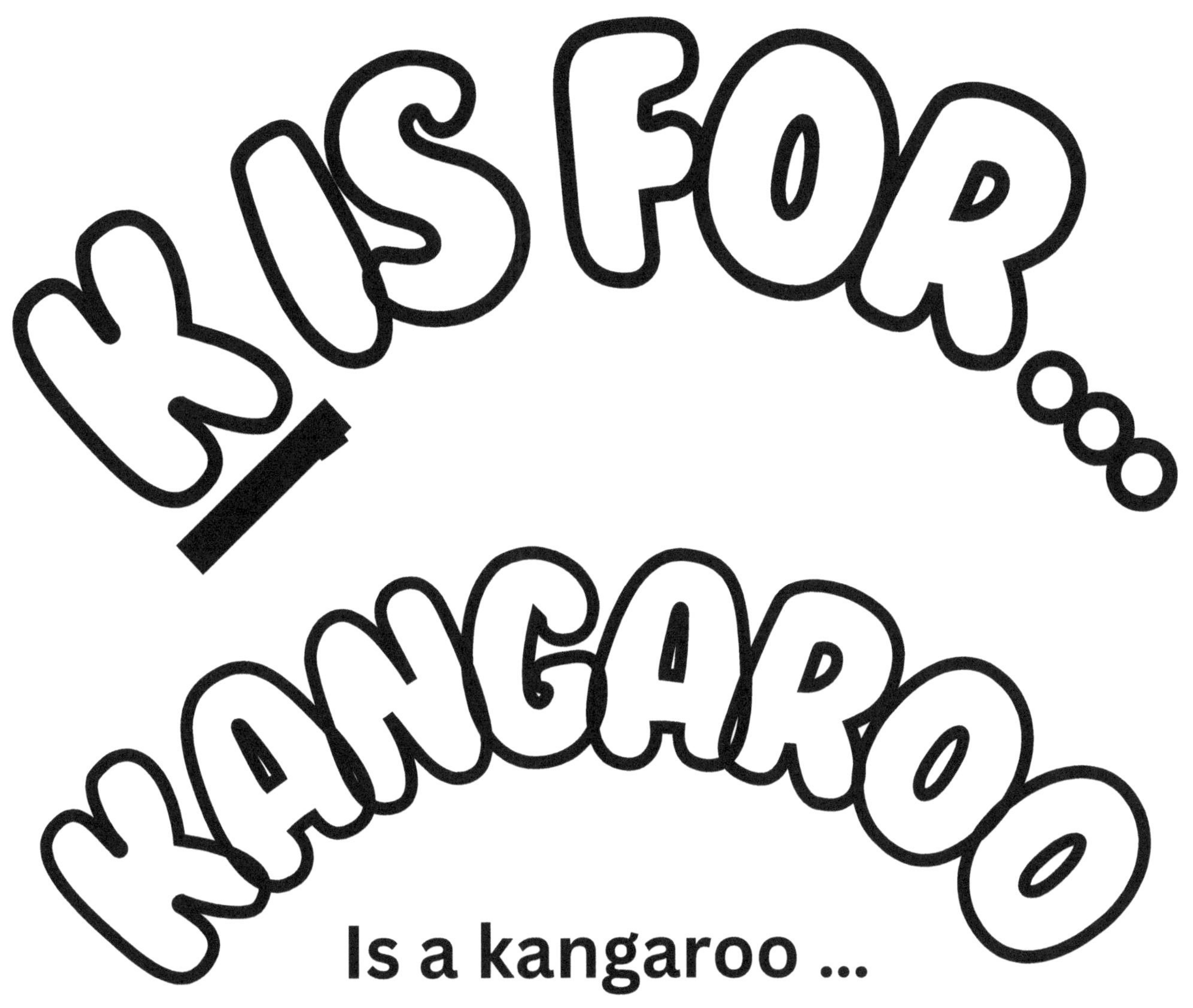

Is a kangaroo ...

a. Cold Blooded
b. Warm Blooded
c. No Blooded

(Answers on last page)

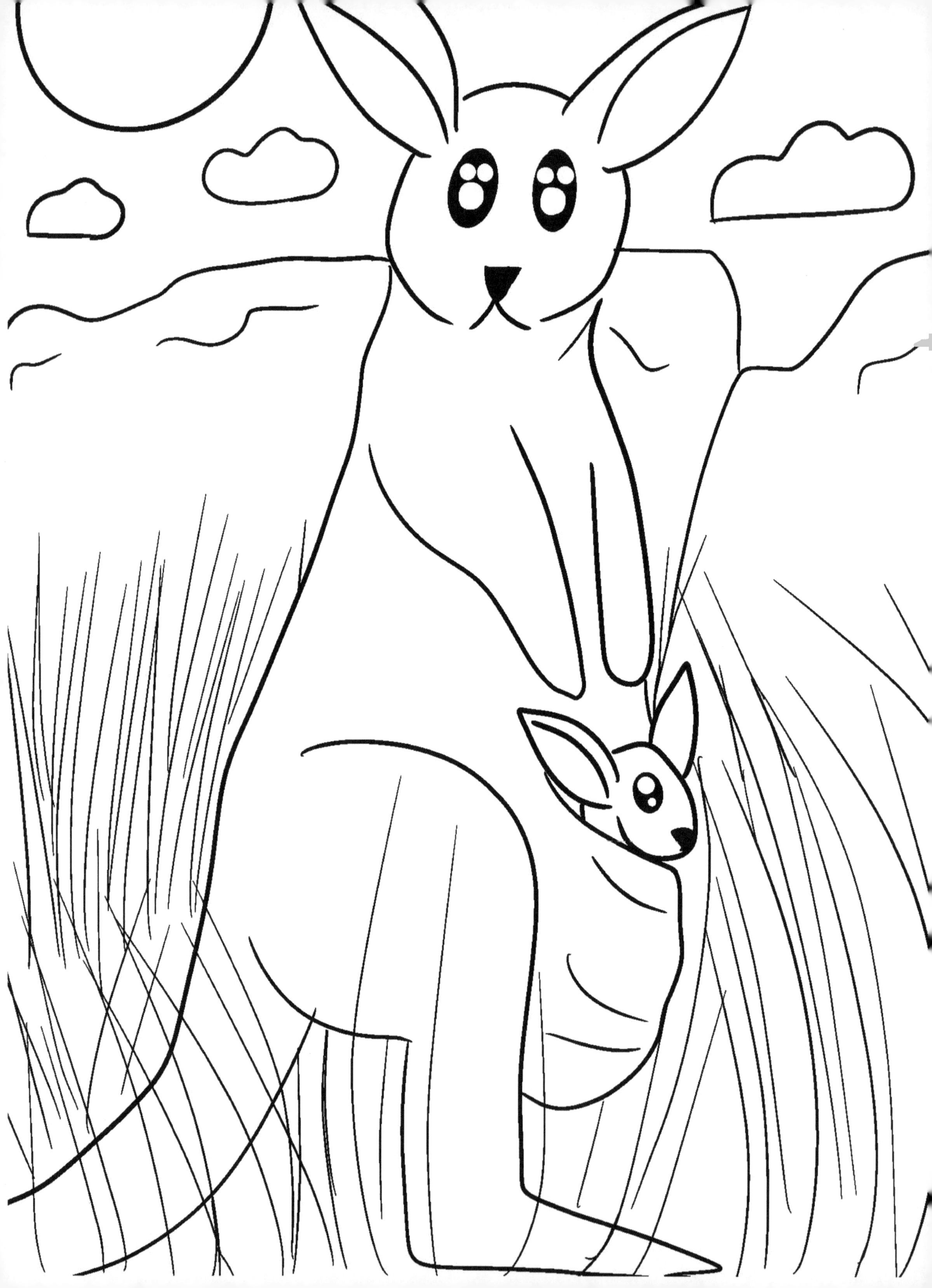

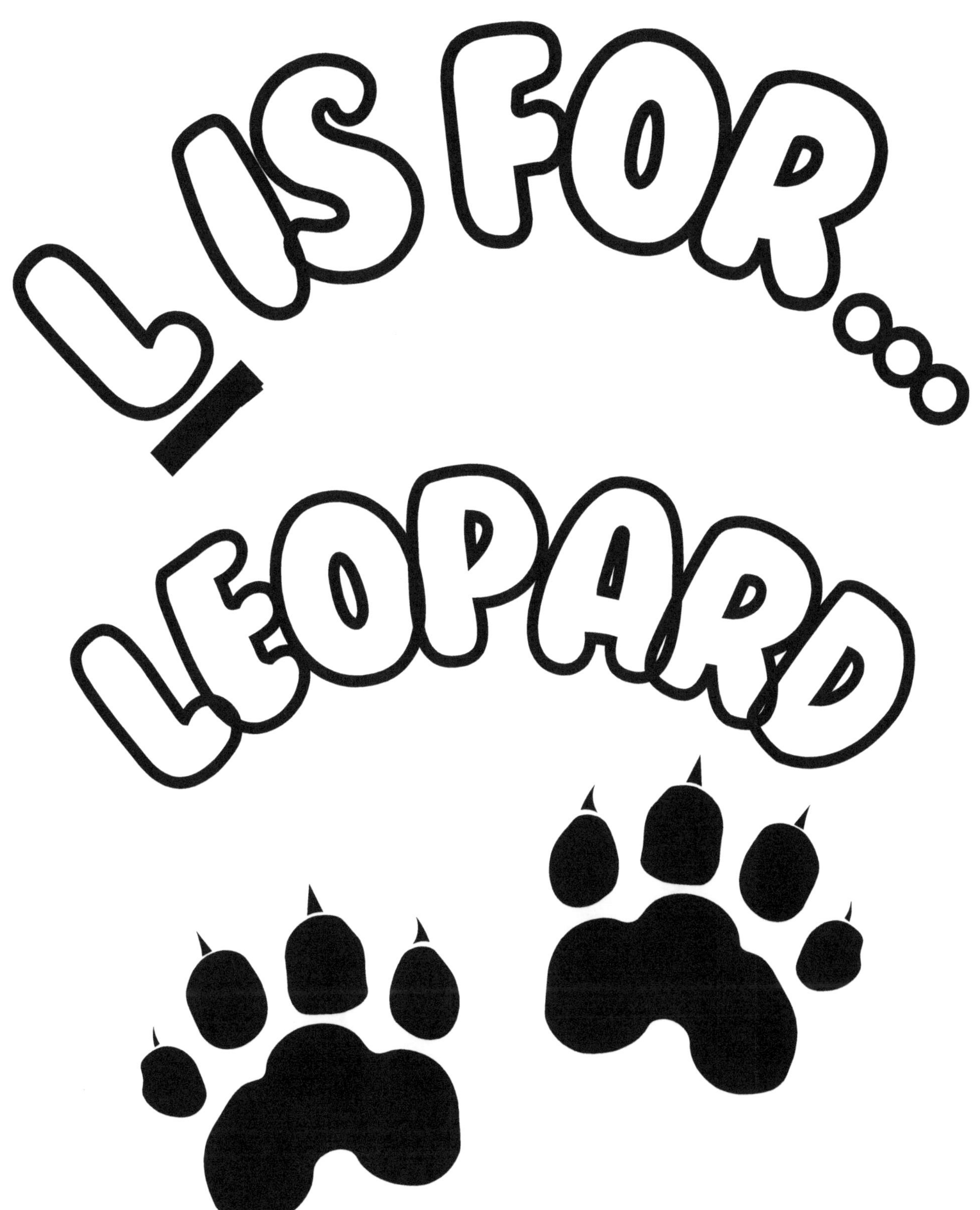

L IS FOR...
LEOPARD

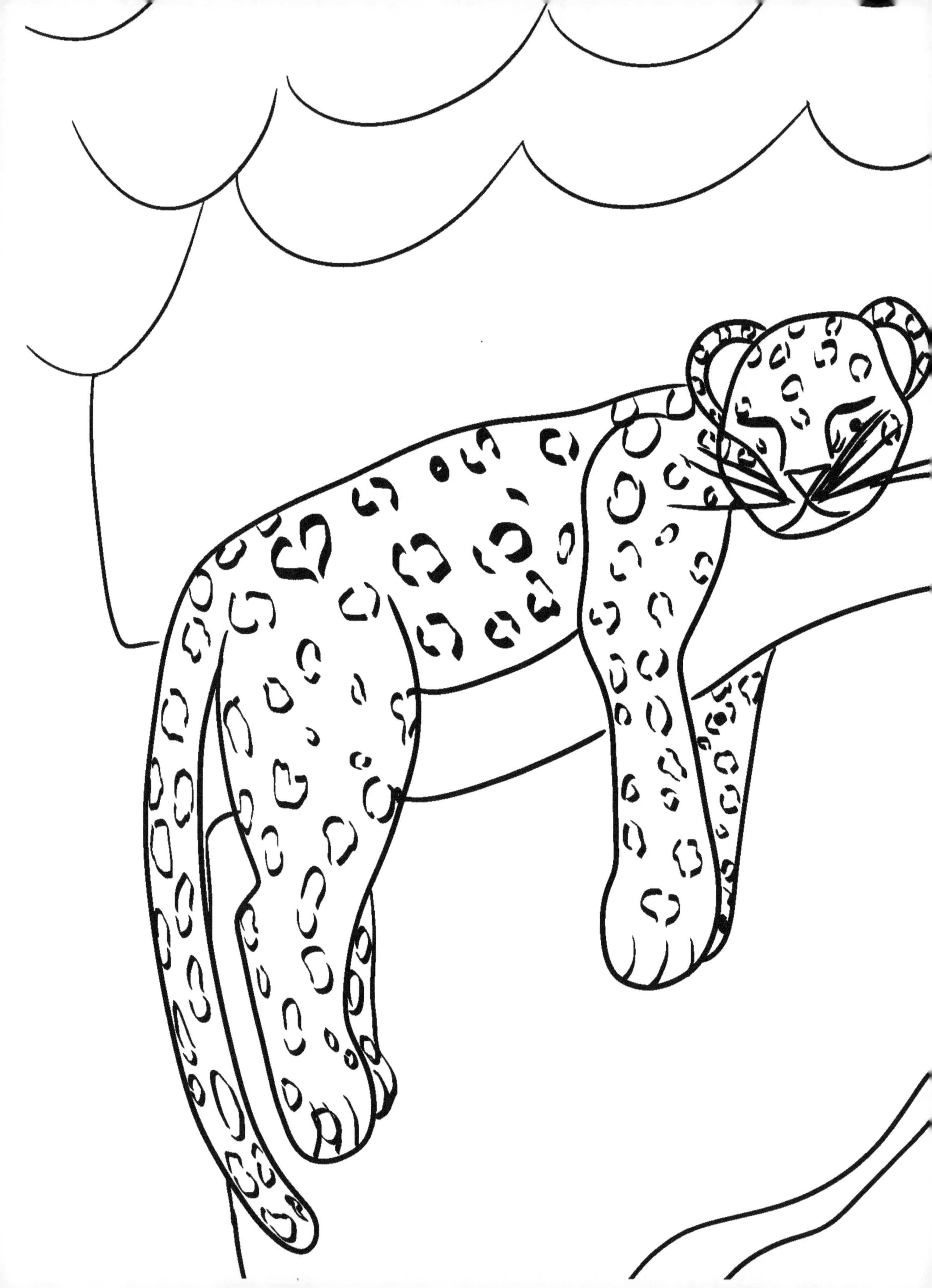

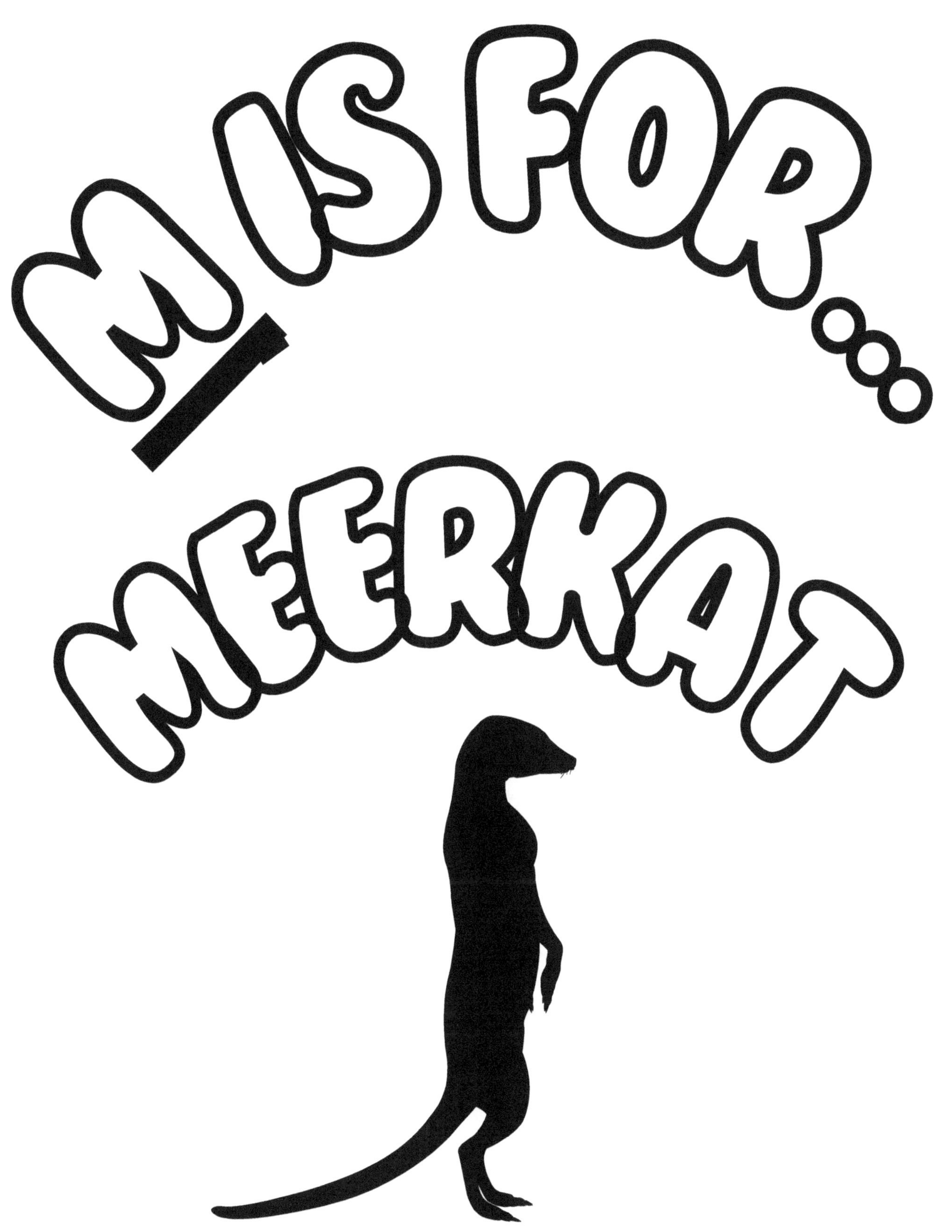

M IS FOR...
MEERKAT

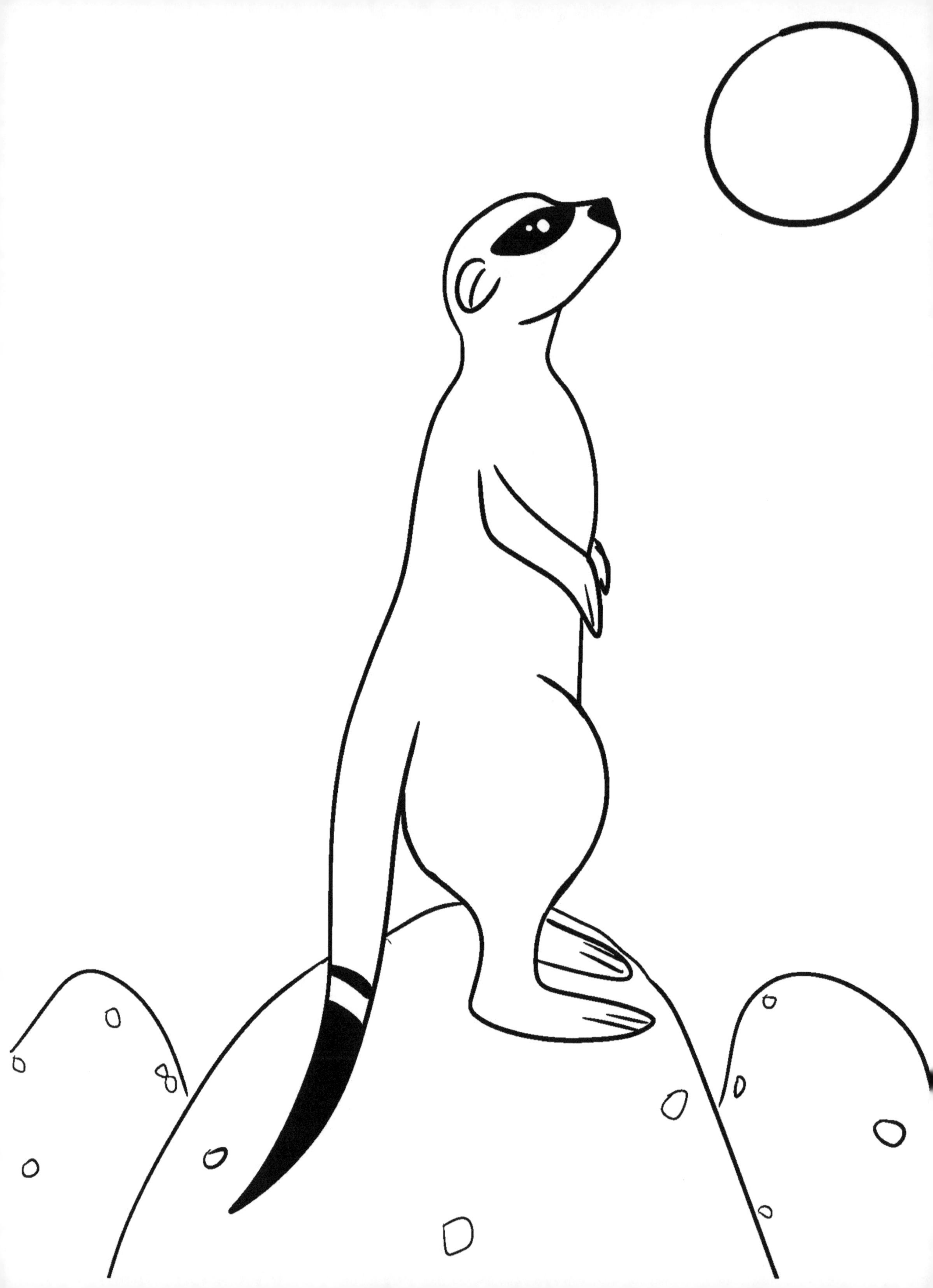

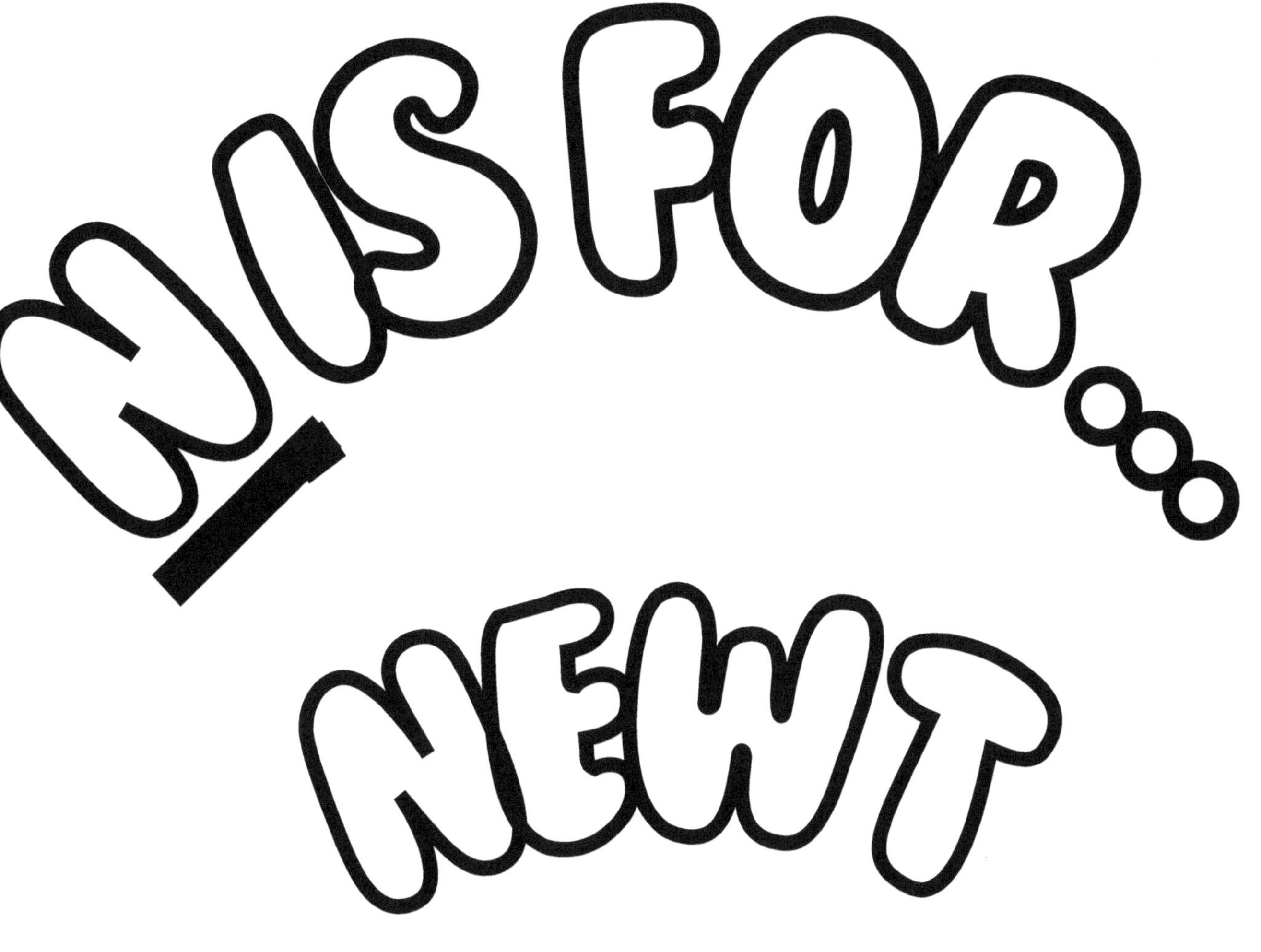

Is a newt a ...

a. Mammal
b. Reptile
c. Fish
d. Amphibian
e. Bird
f. Bug

(Answers on last page)

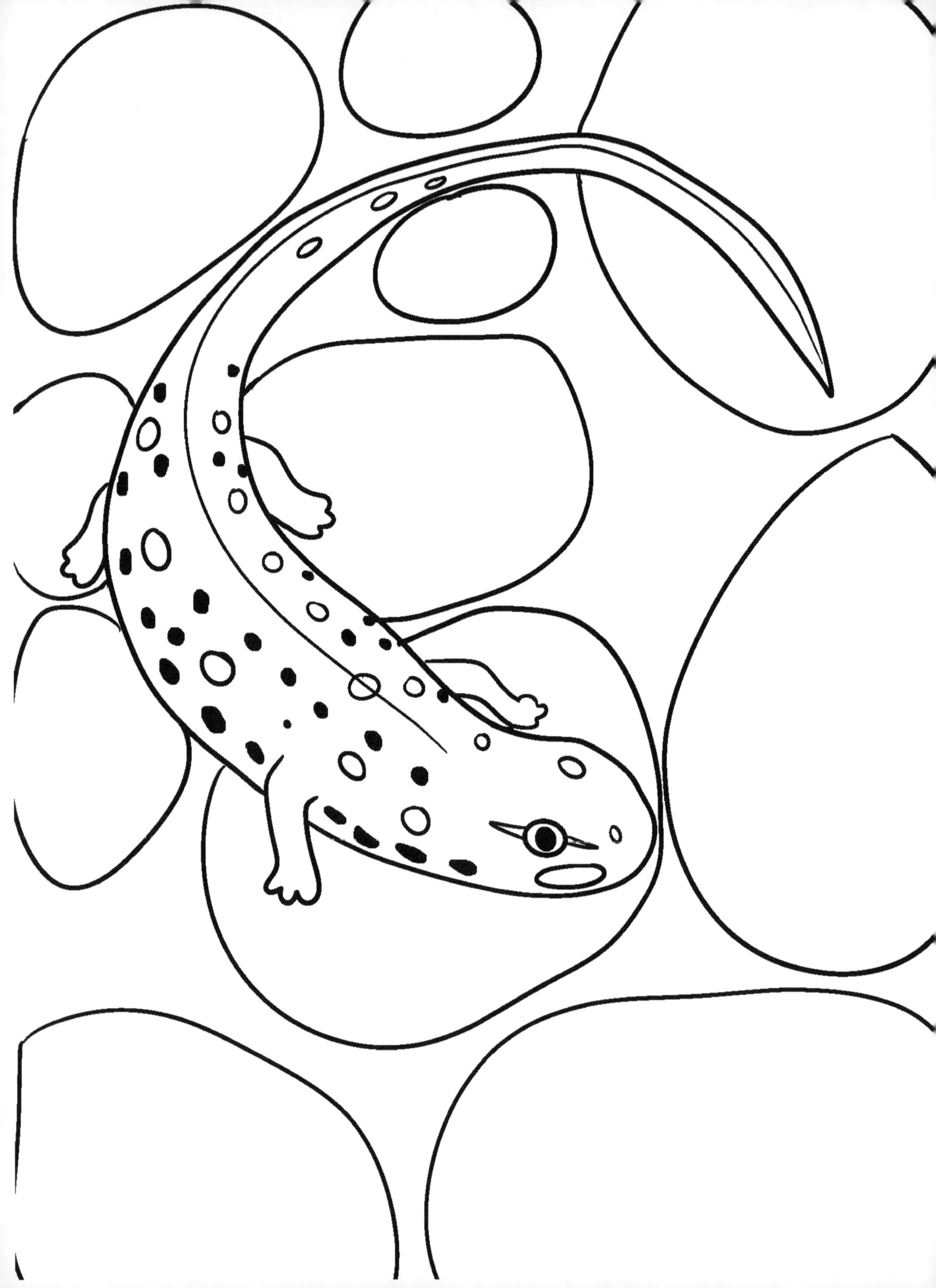

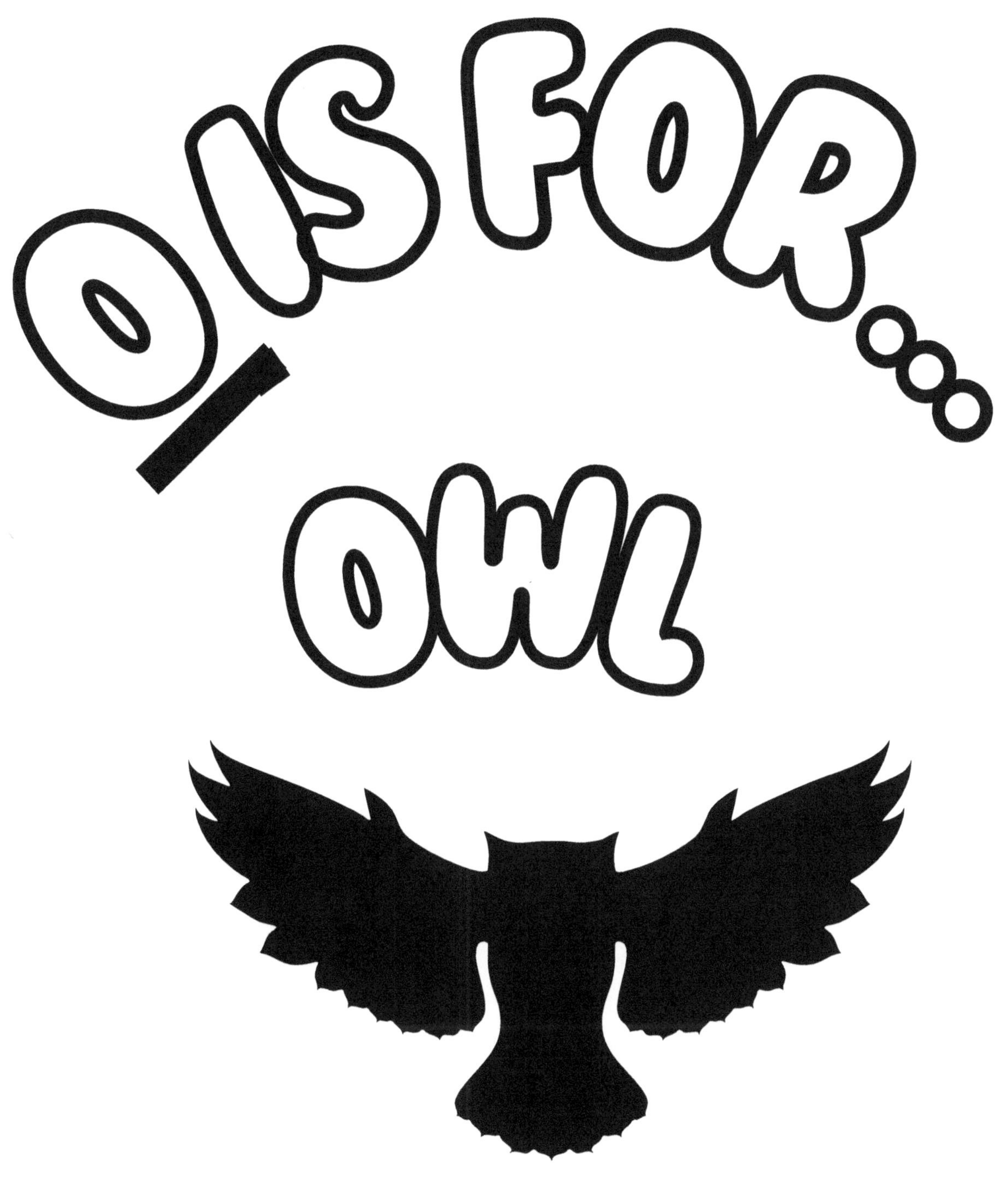

(Answers on last page)

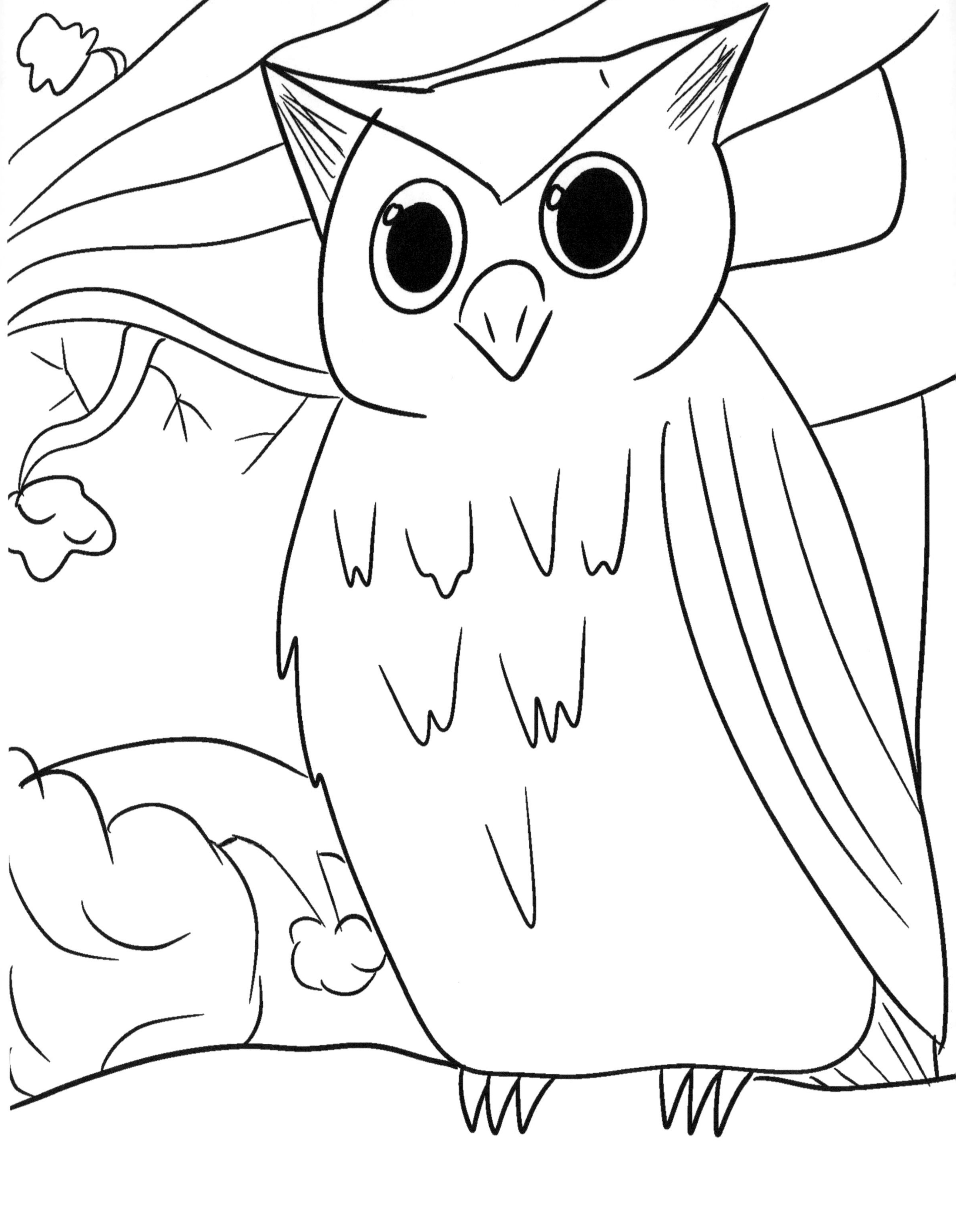

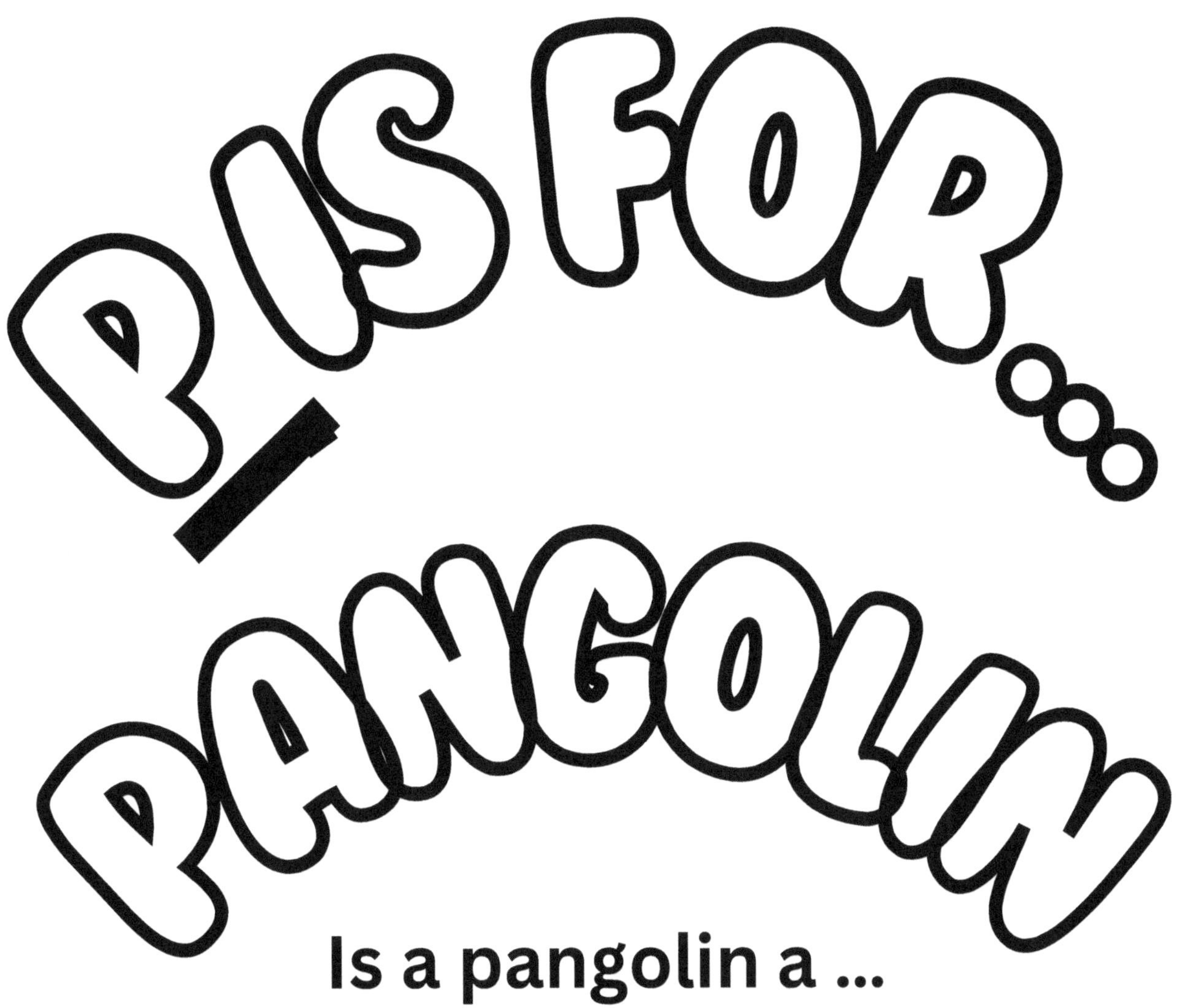

Is a pangolin a ...

a. Mammal
b. Reptile
c. Fish
d. Amphibian
e. Bird
f. Bug

(Answers on last page)

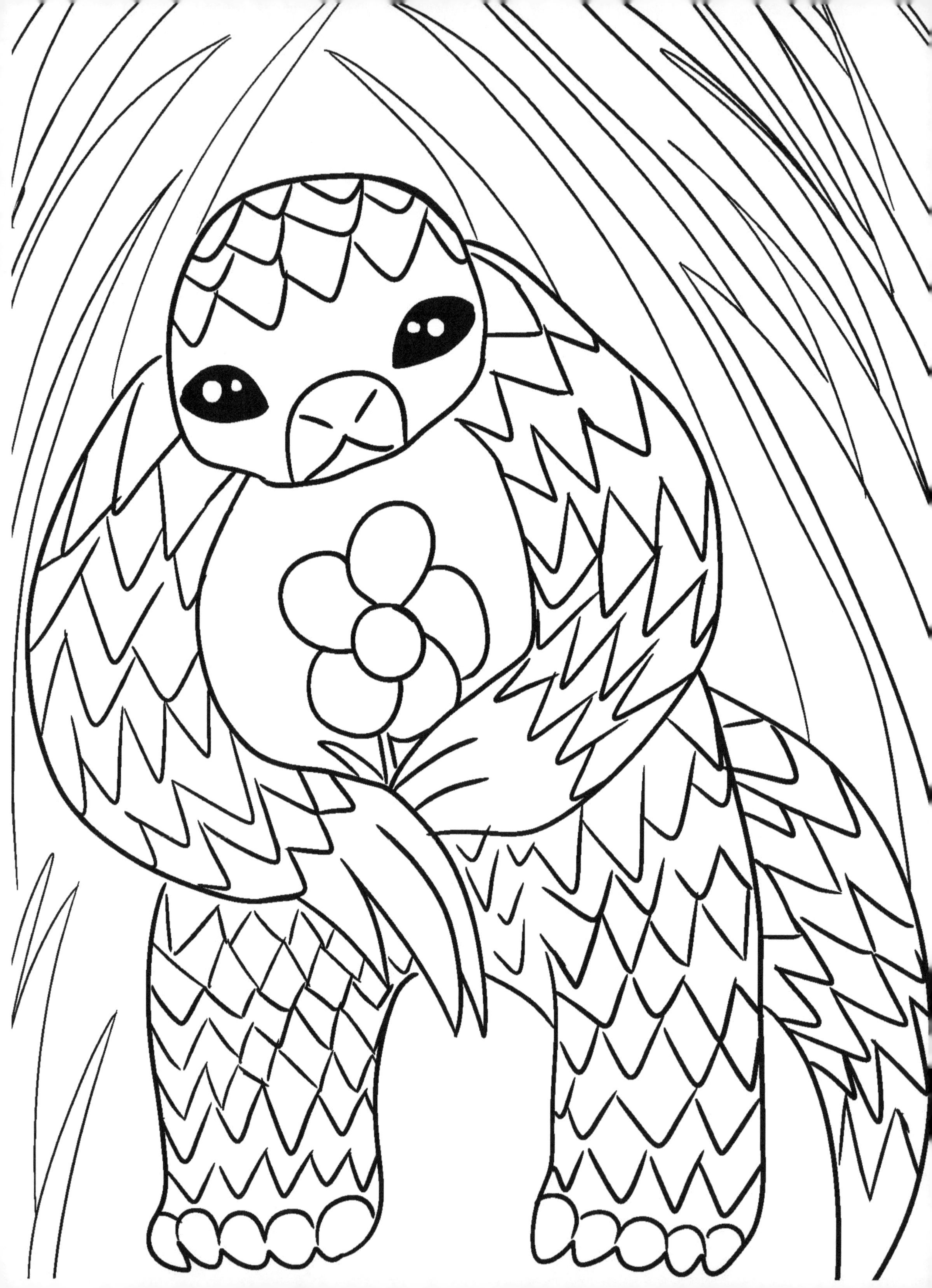

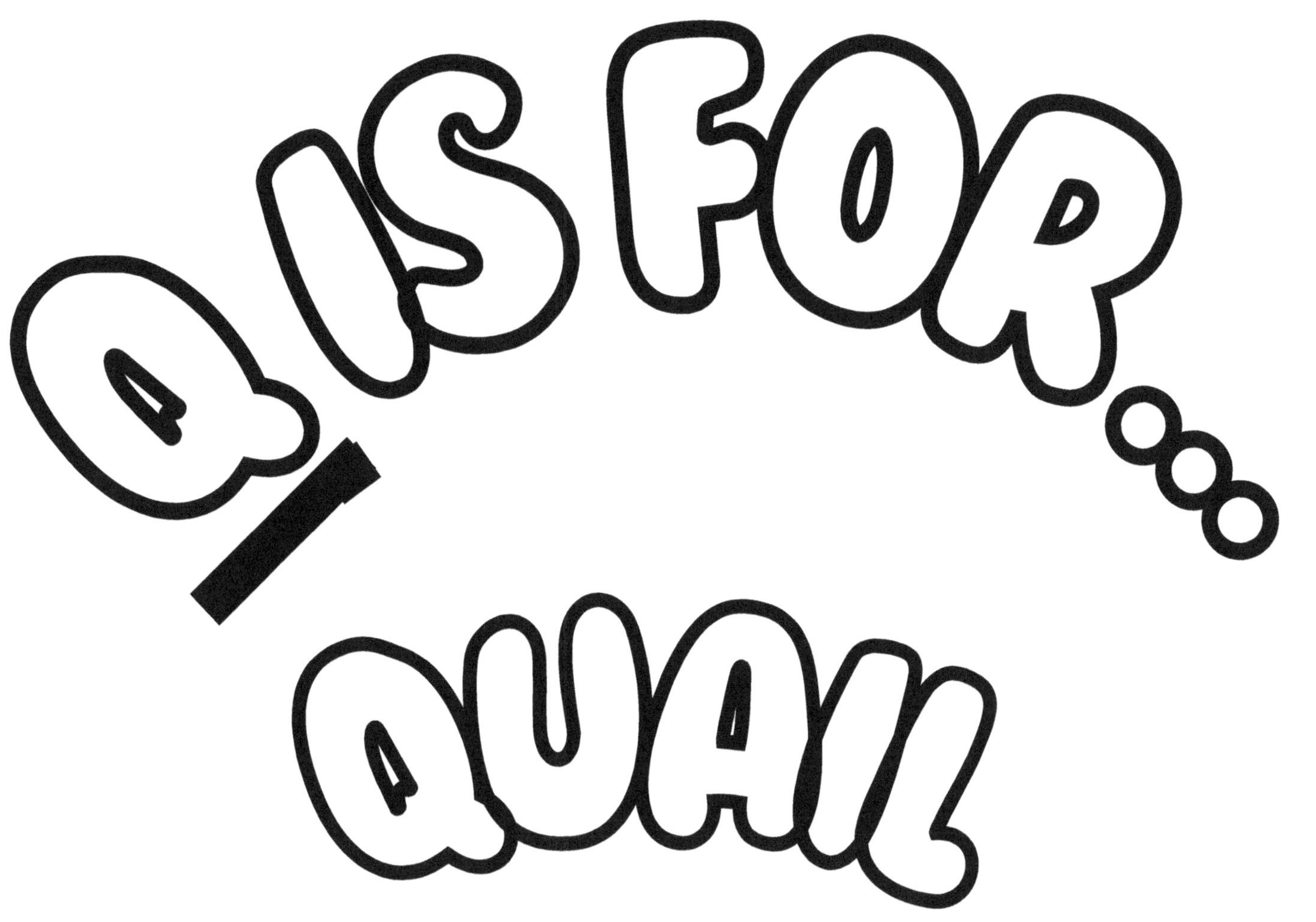

Is a quail a ...

a. Mammal
b. Reptile
c. Fish
d. Amphibian
e. Bird
f. Bug

(Answers on last page)

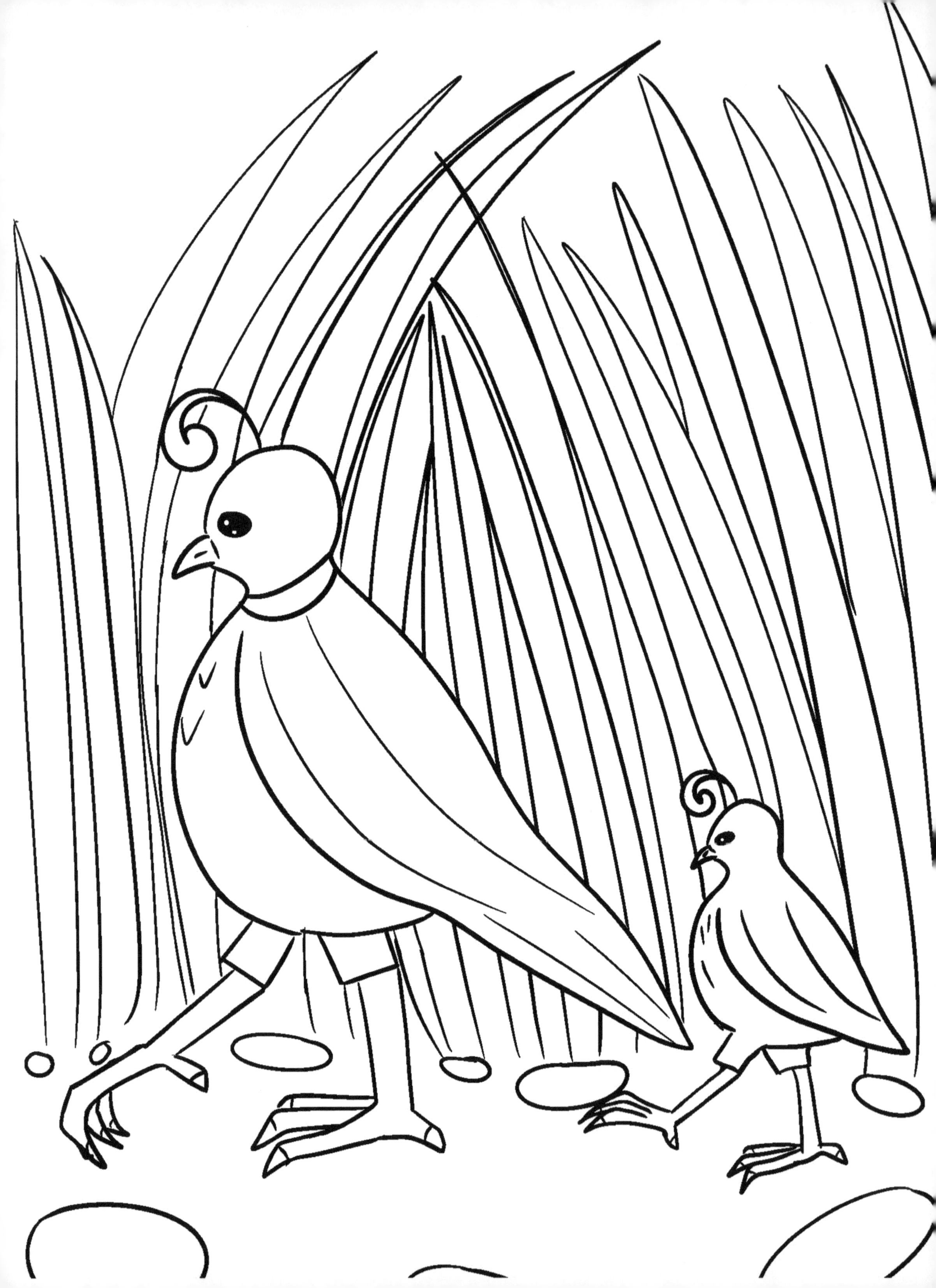

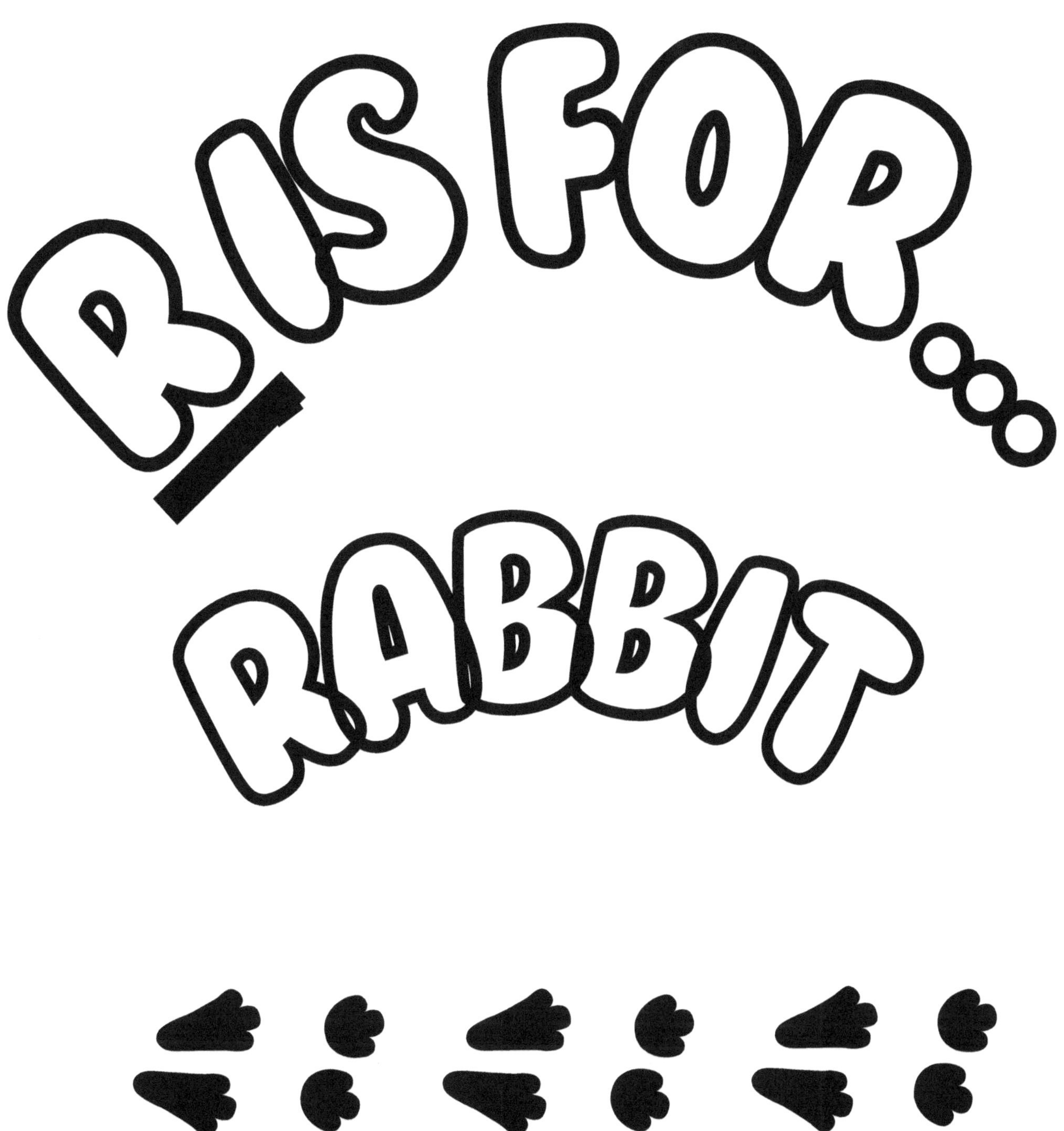

R IS FOR...
RABBIT

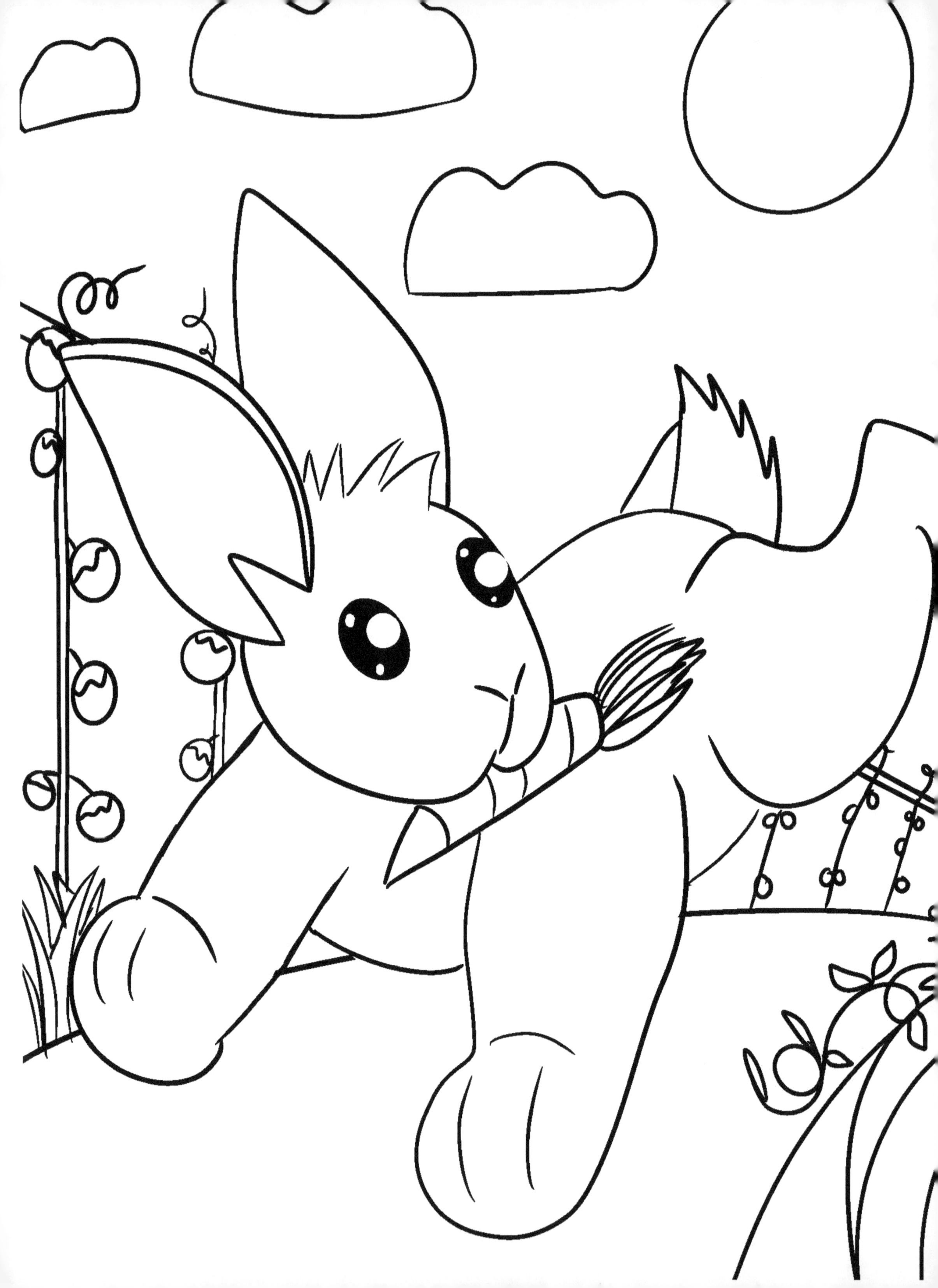

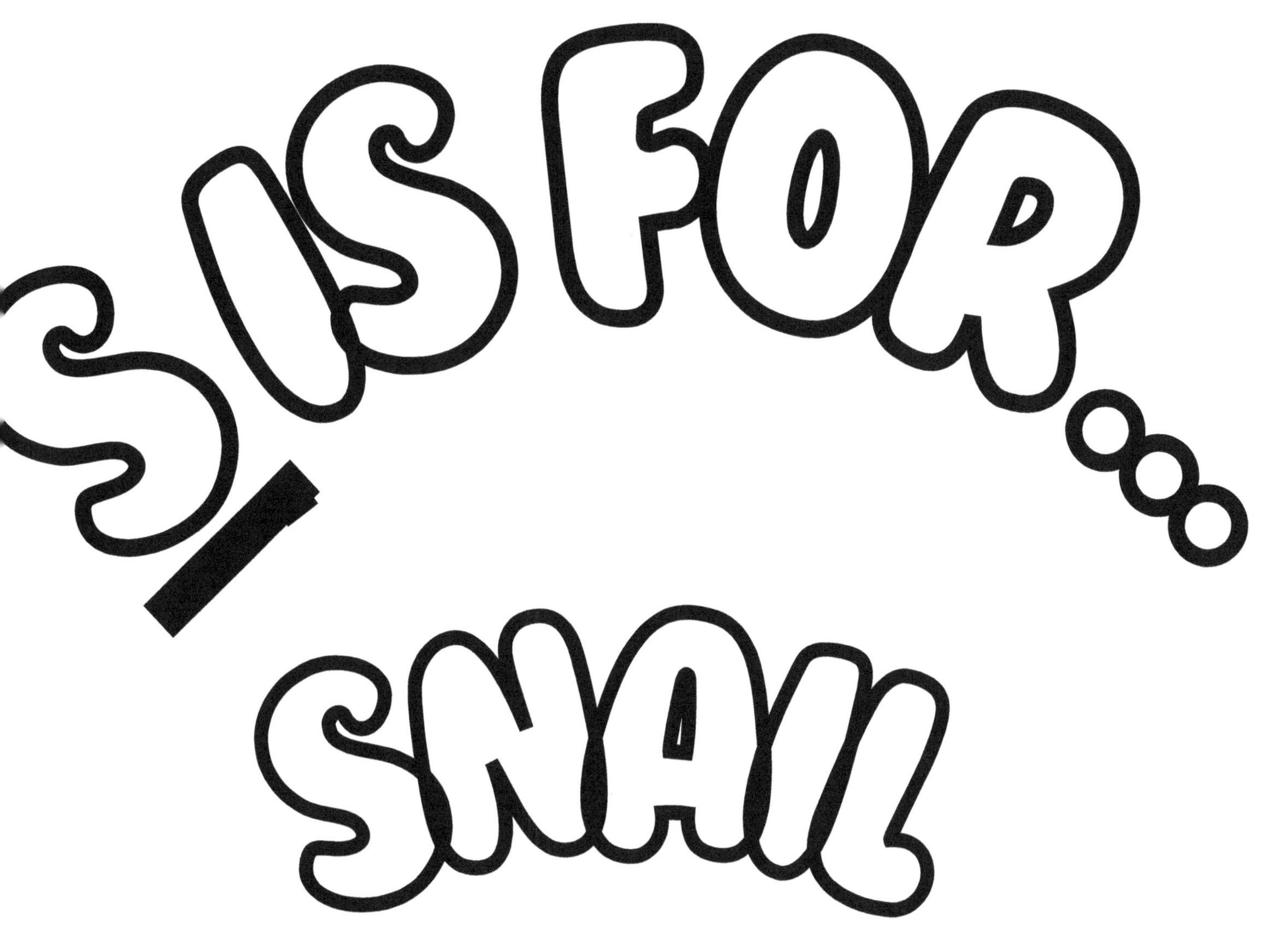

Is a snail a ...

a. Mammal
b. Reptile
c. Fish
d. Amphibian
e. Bird
f. Bug

(Answers on last page)

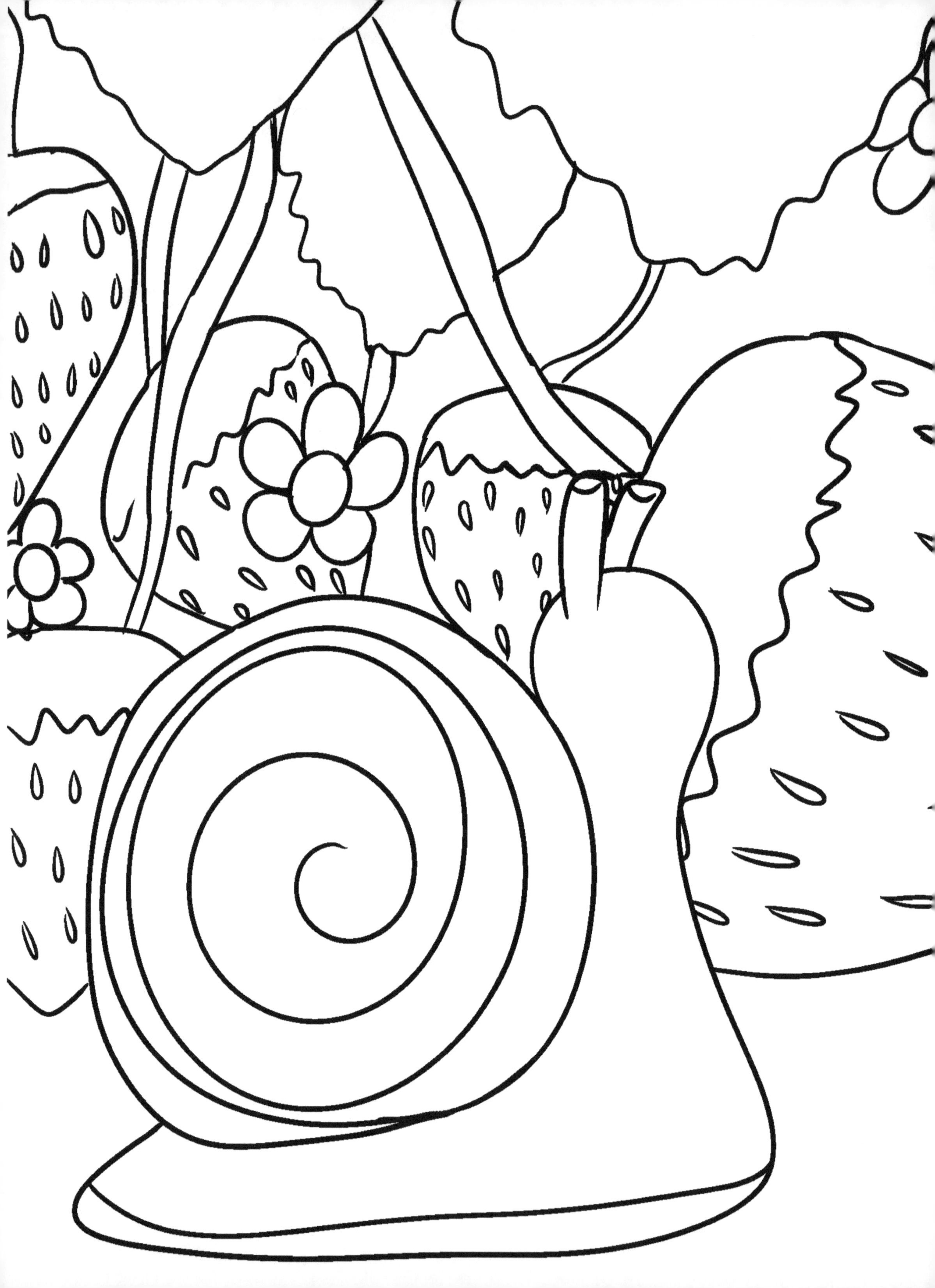

I IS FOR...

TIGERS

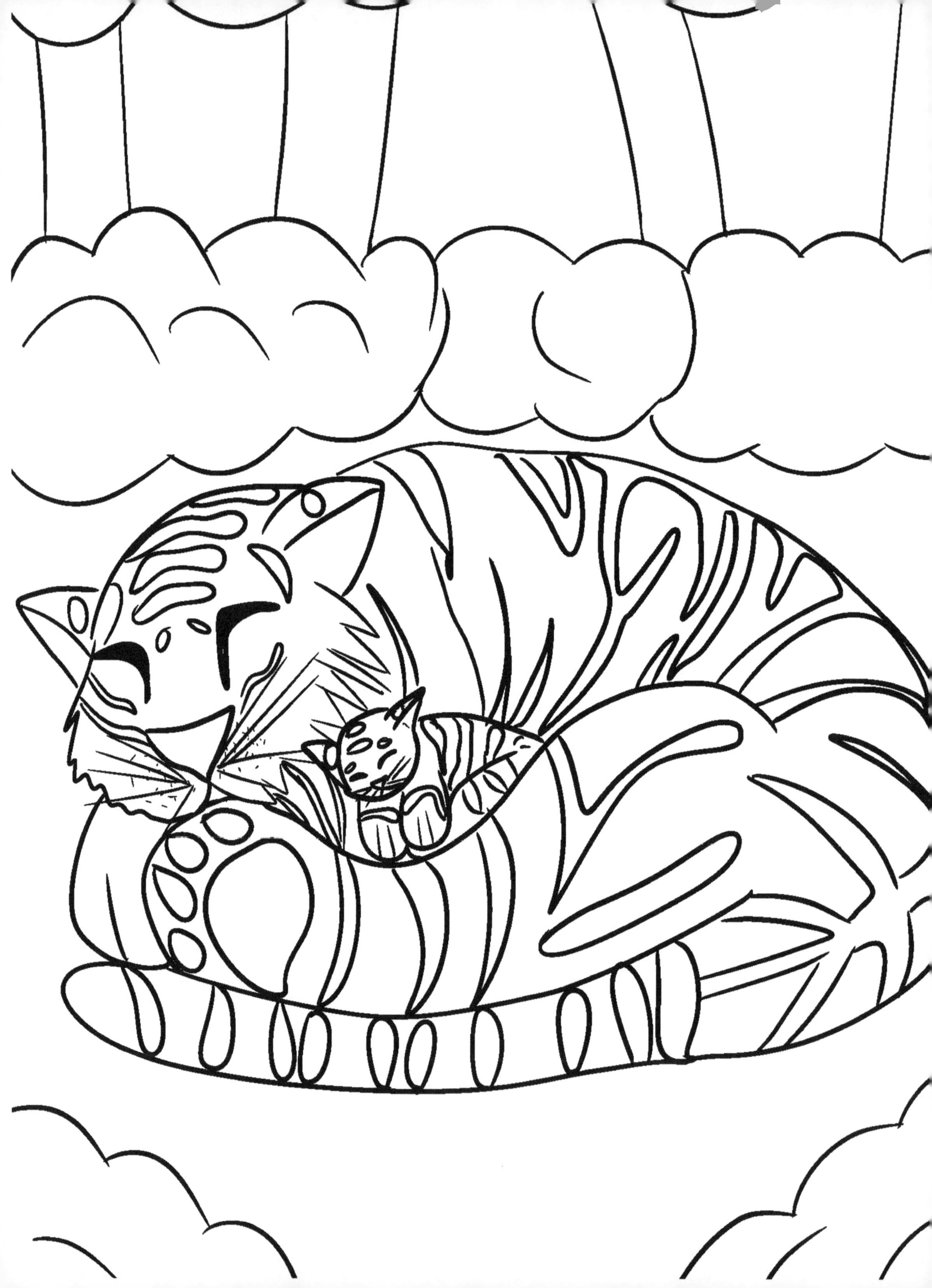

U IS FOR... URCHINS

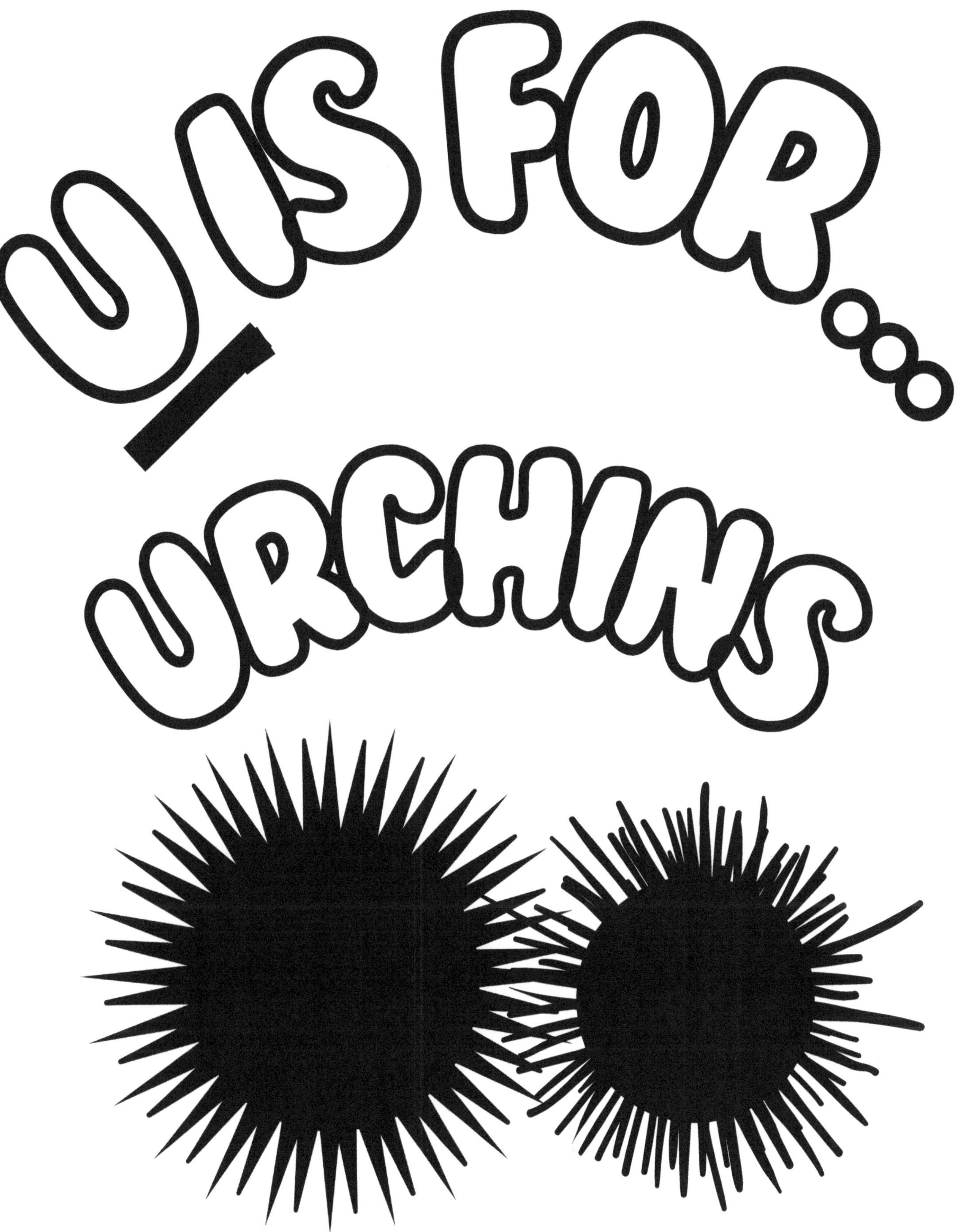

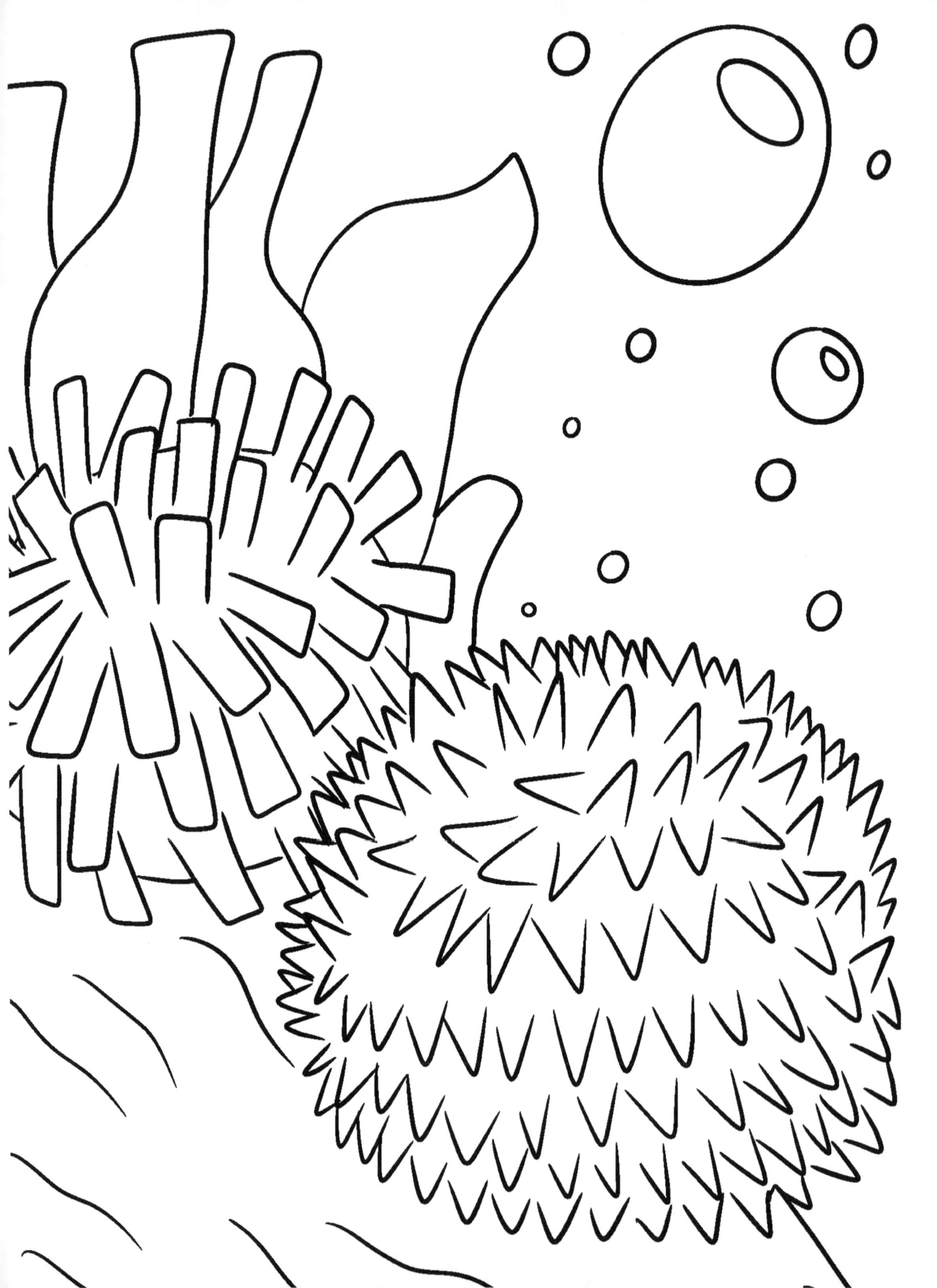

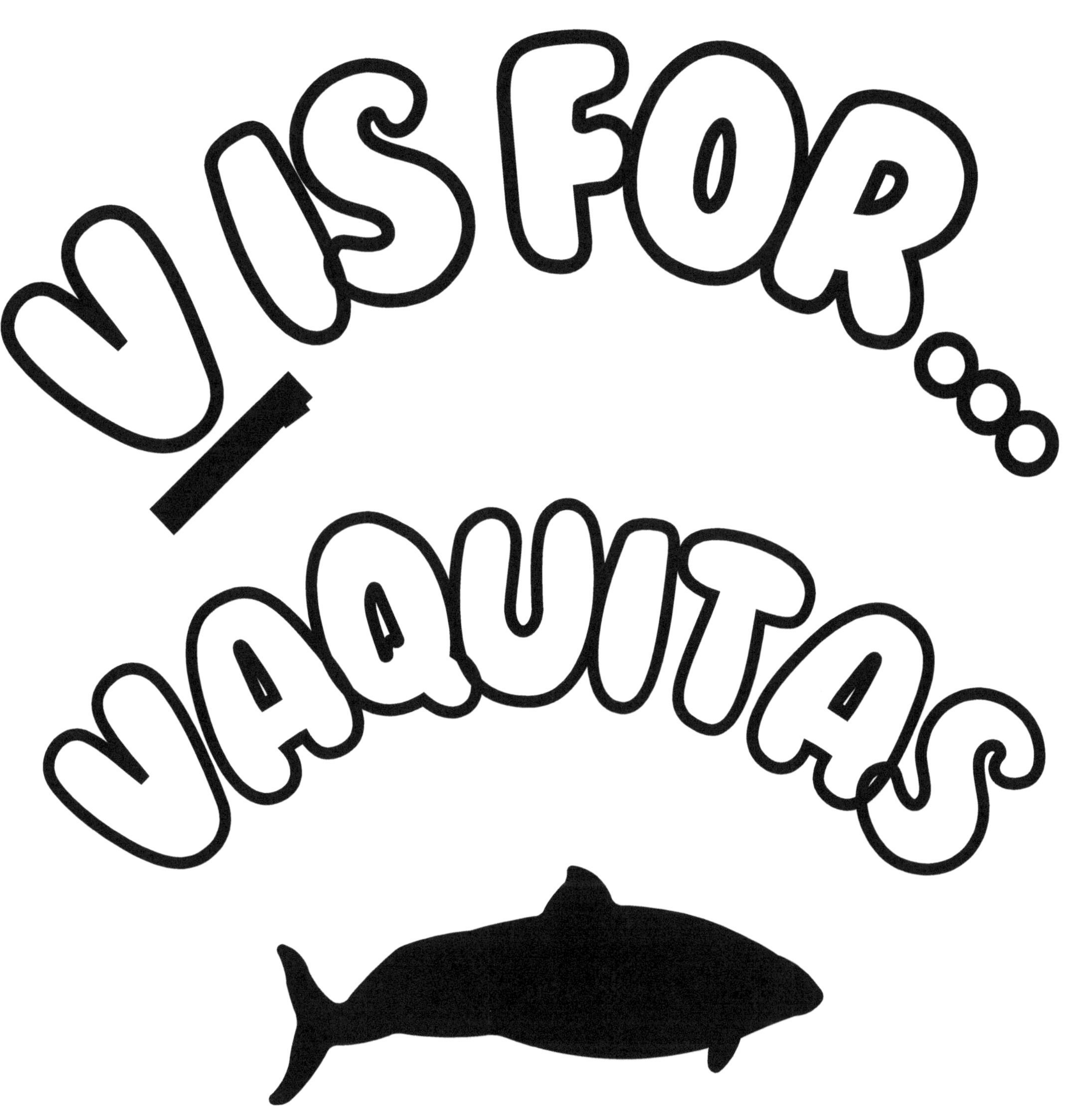
V IS FOR...
VAQUITAS

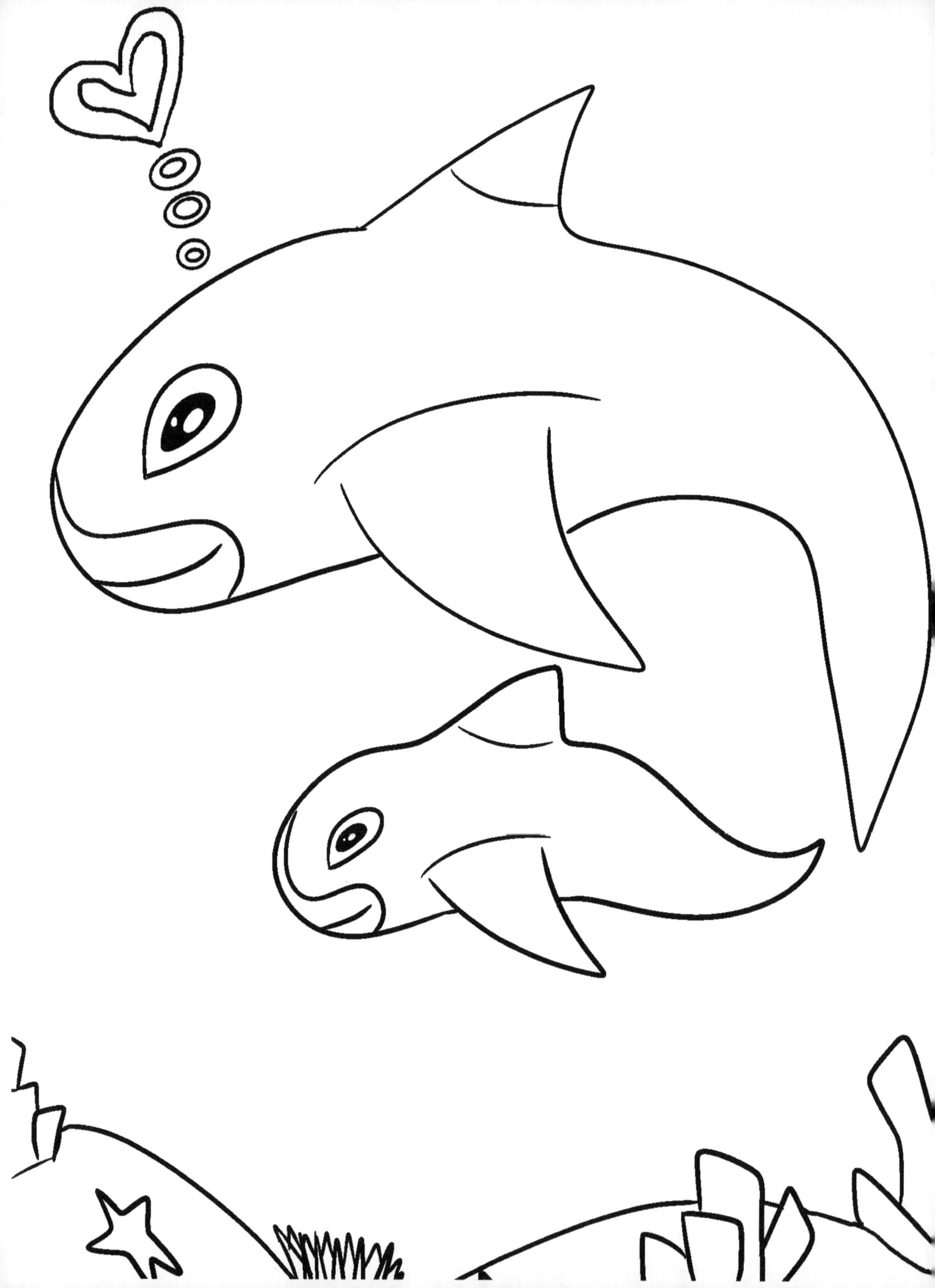

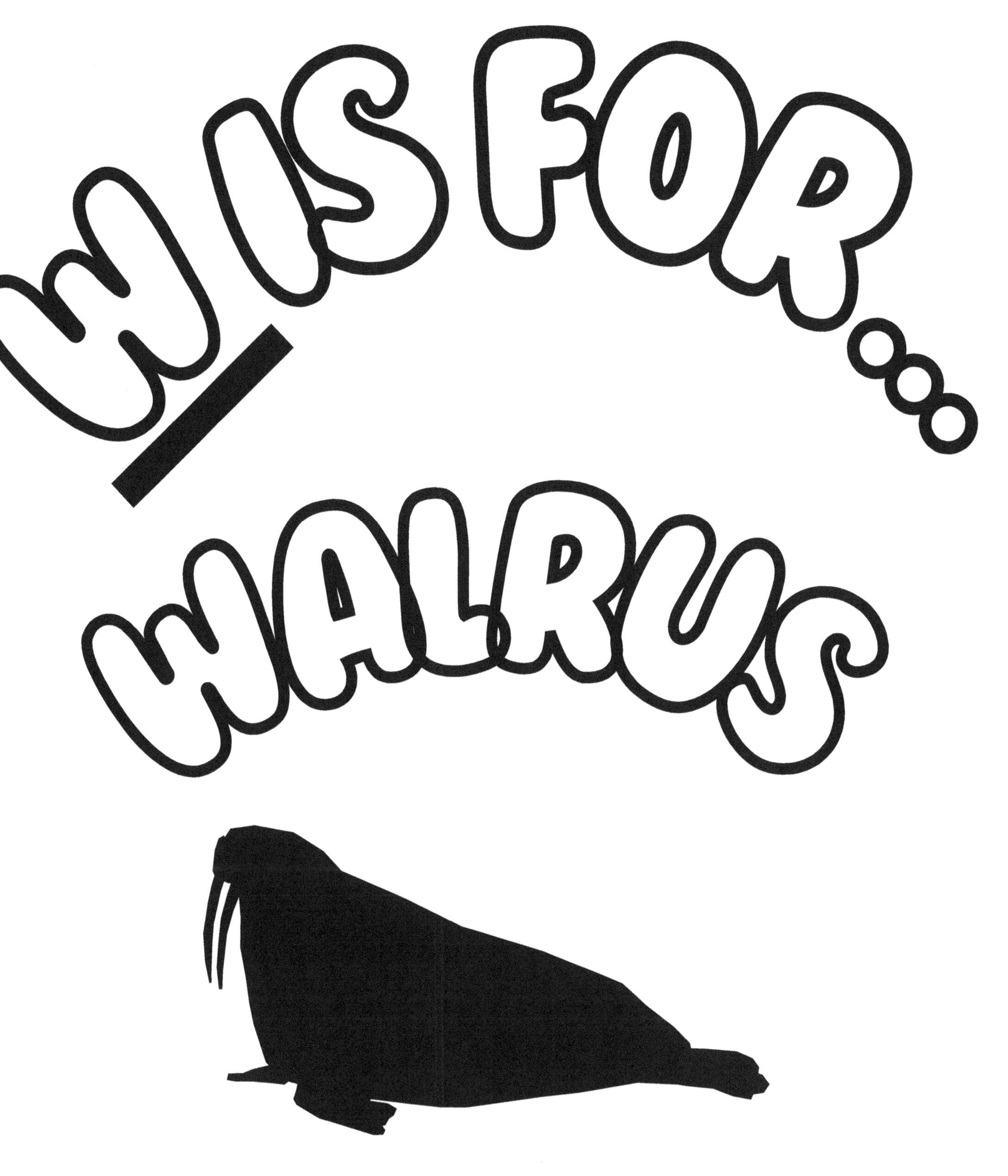

W IS FOR...
WALRUS

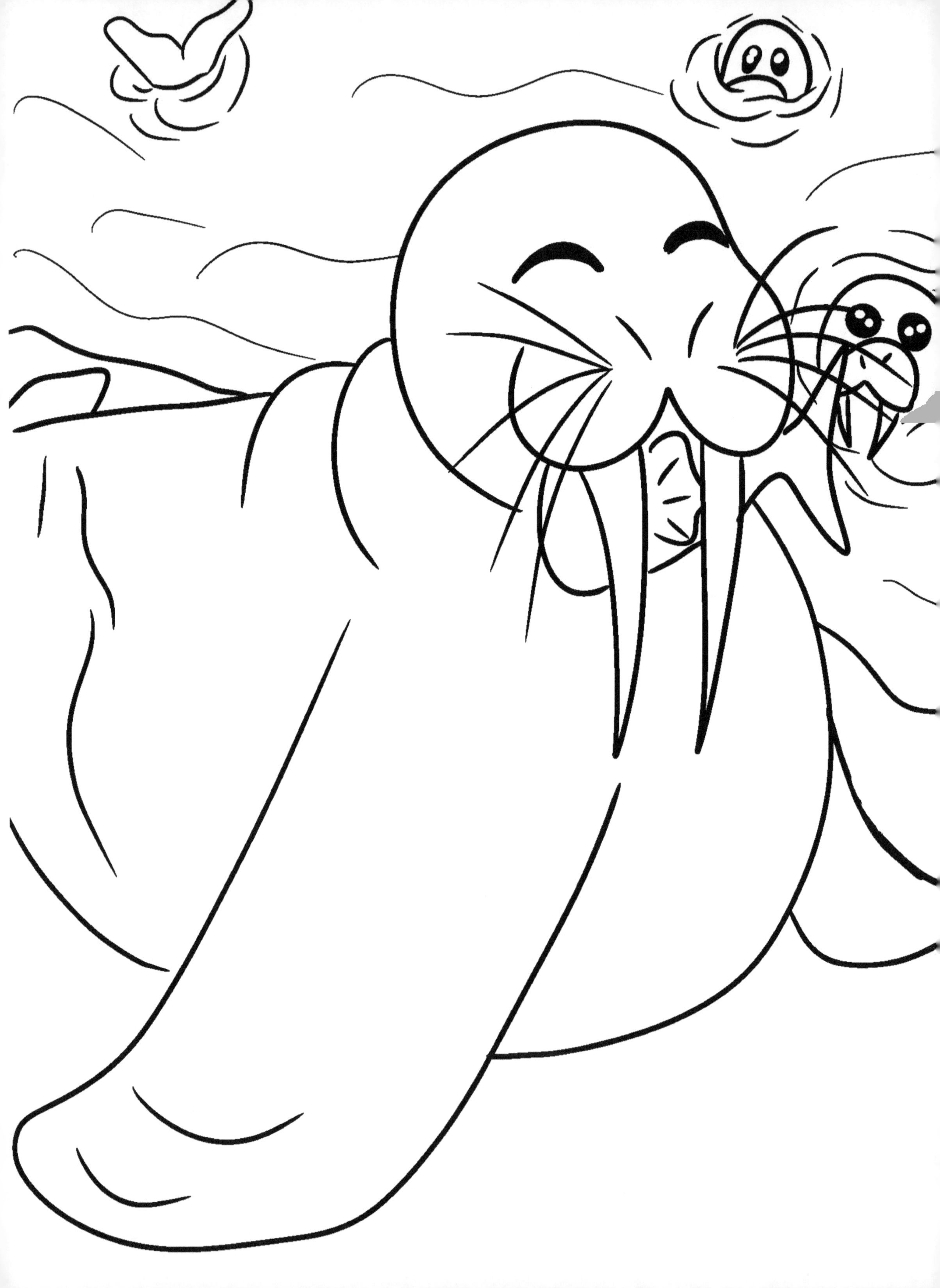

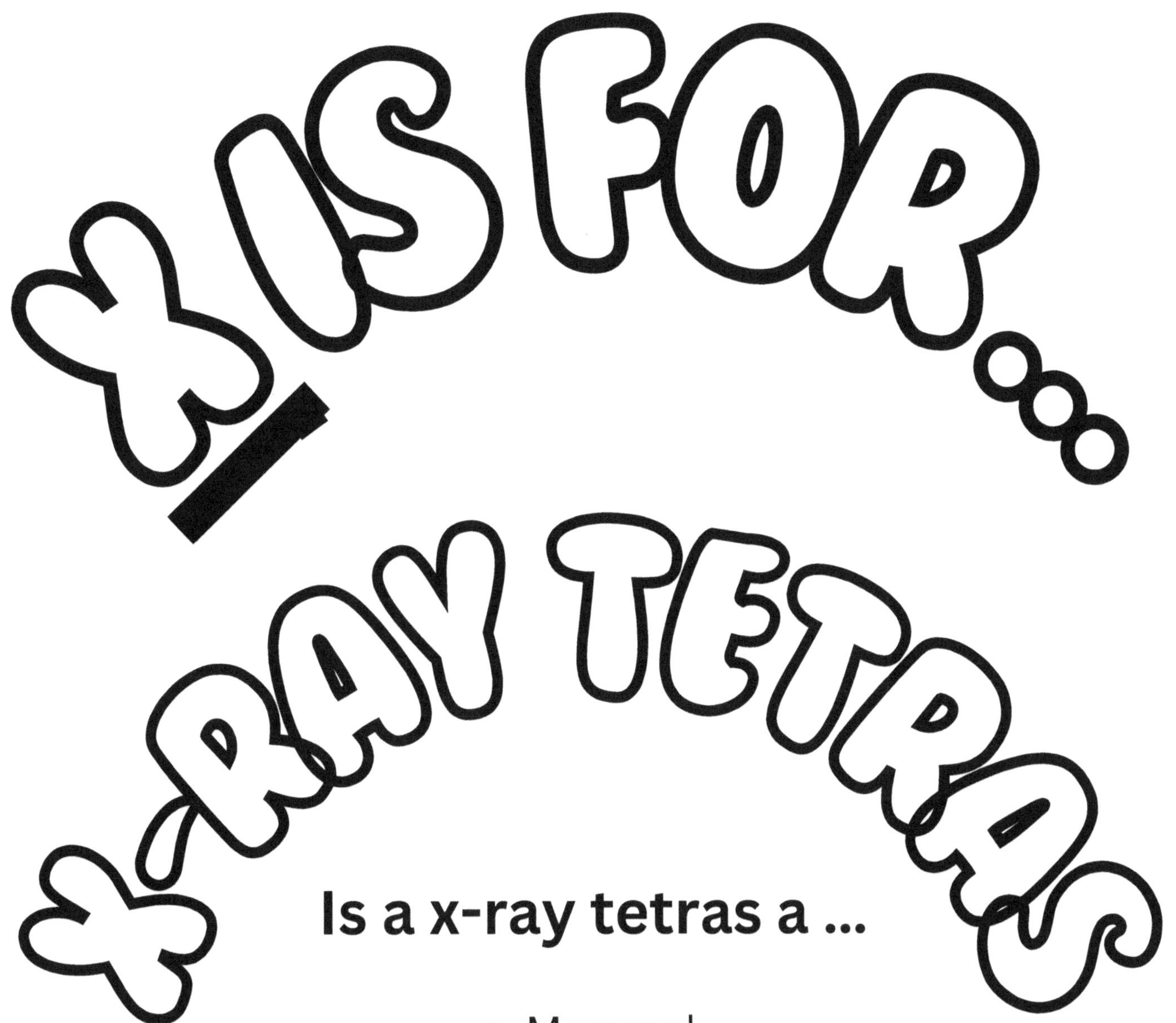

Is a x-ray tetras a ...

a. Mammal
b. Reptile
c. Fish
d. Amphibian
e. Bird
f. Bug

(Answers on last page)

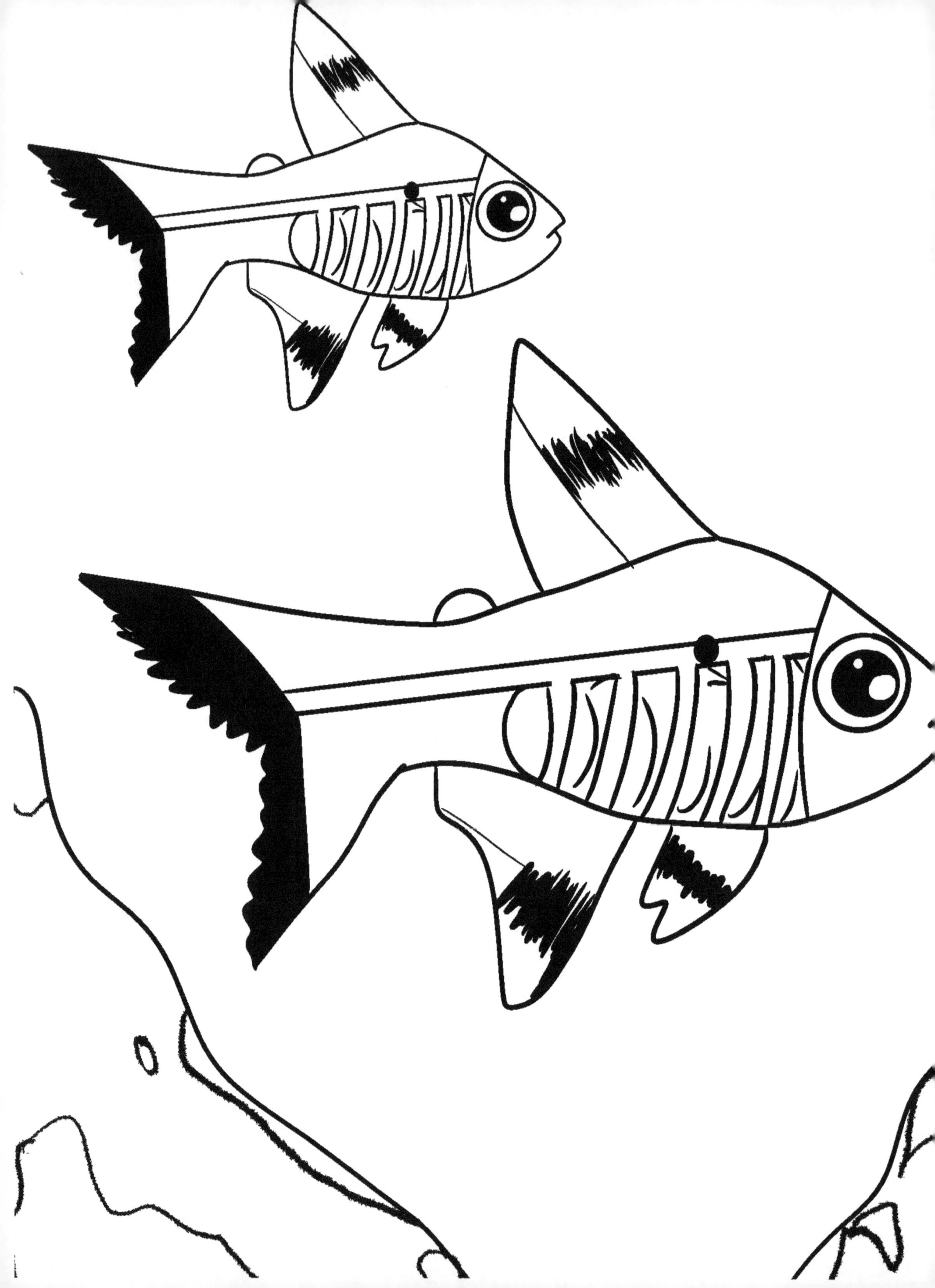

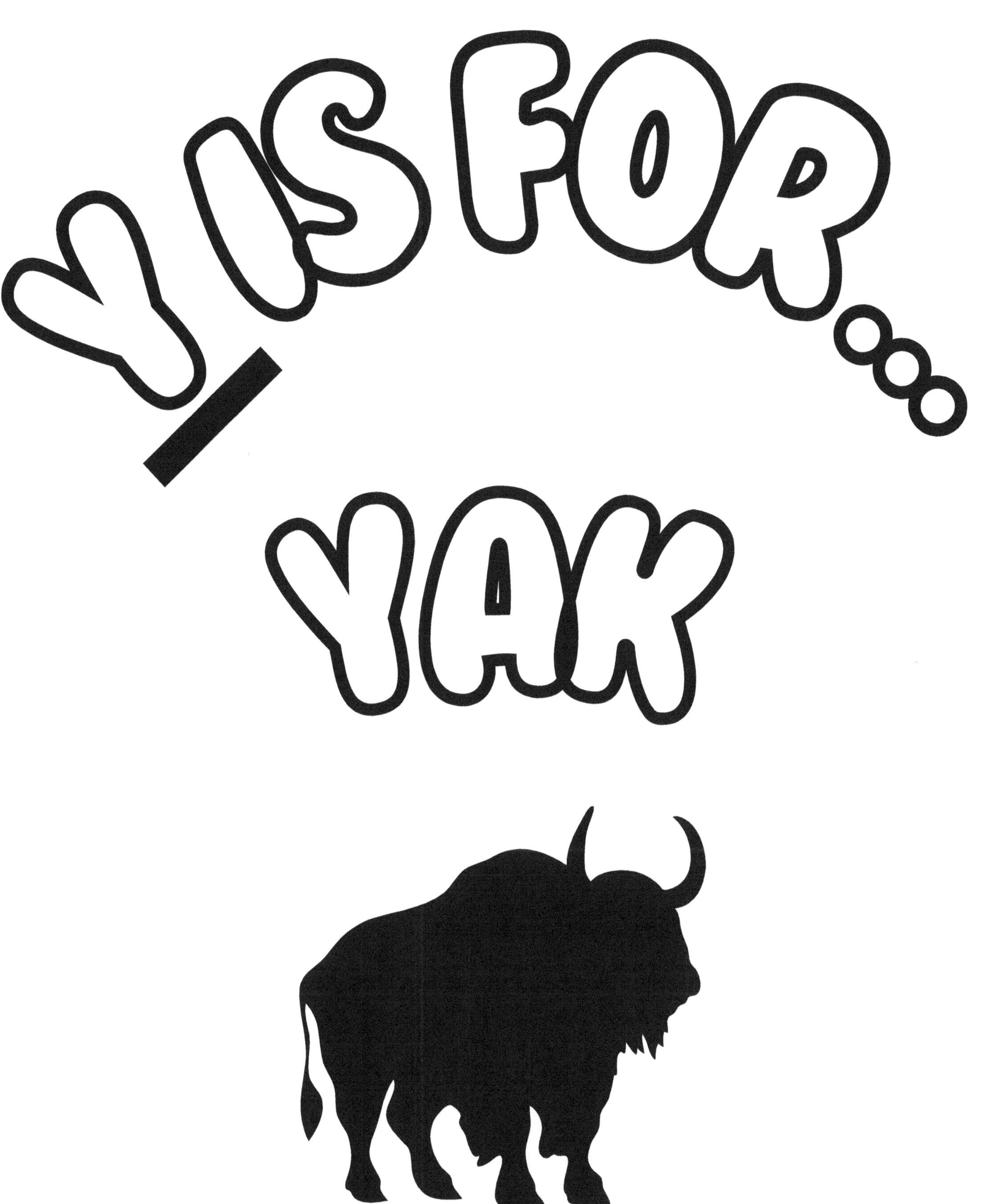
Y IS FOR...
YAK

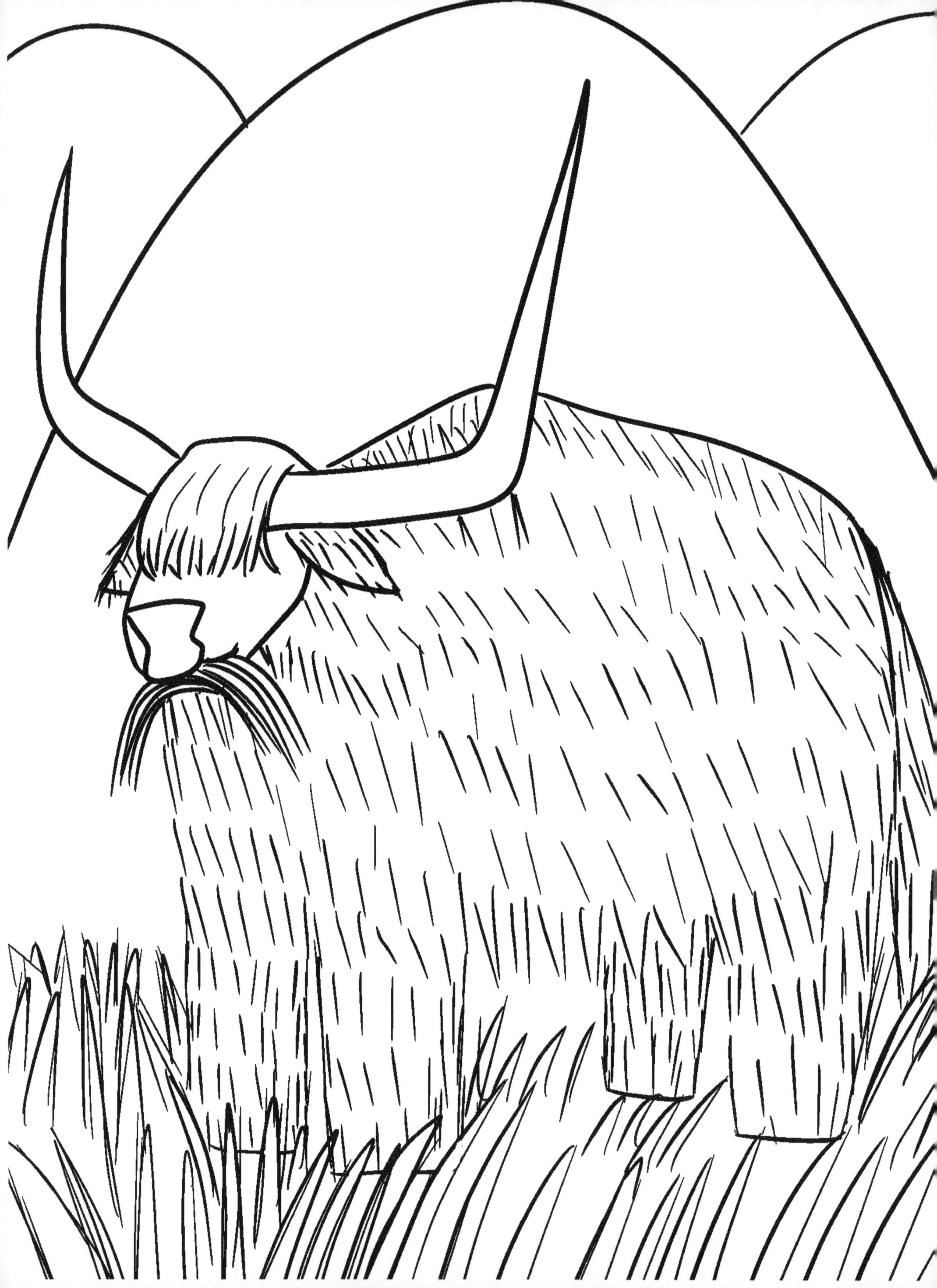

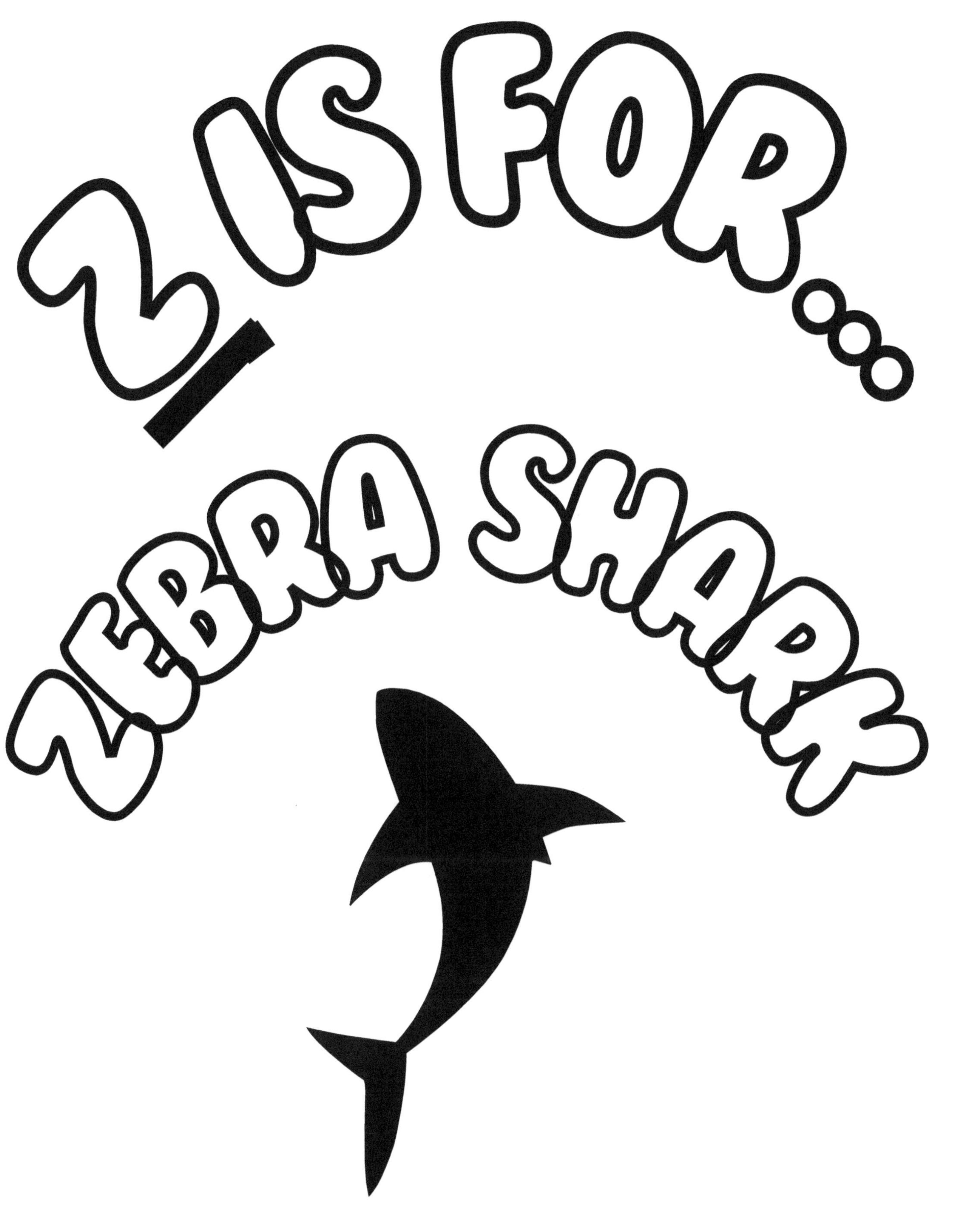

Z IS FOR...
ZEBRA SHARK

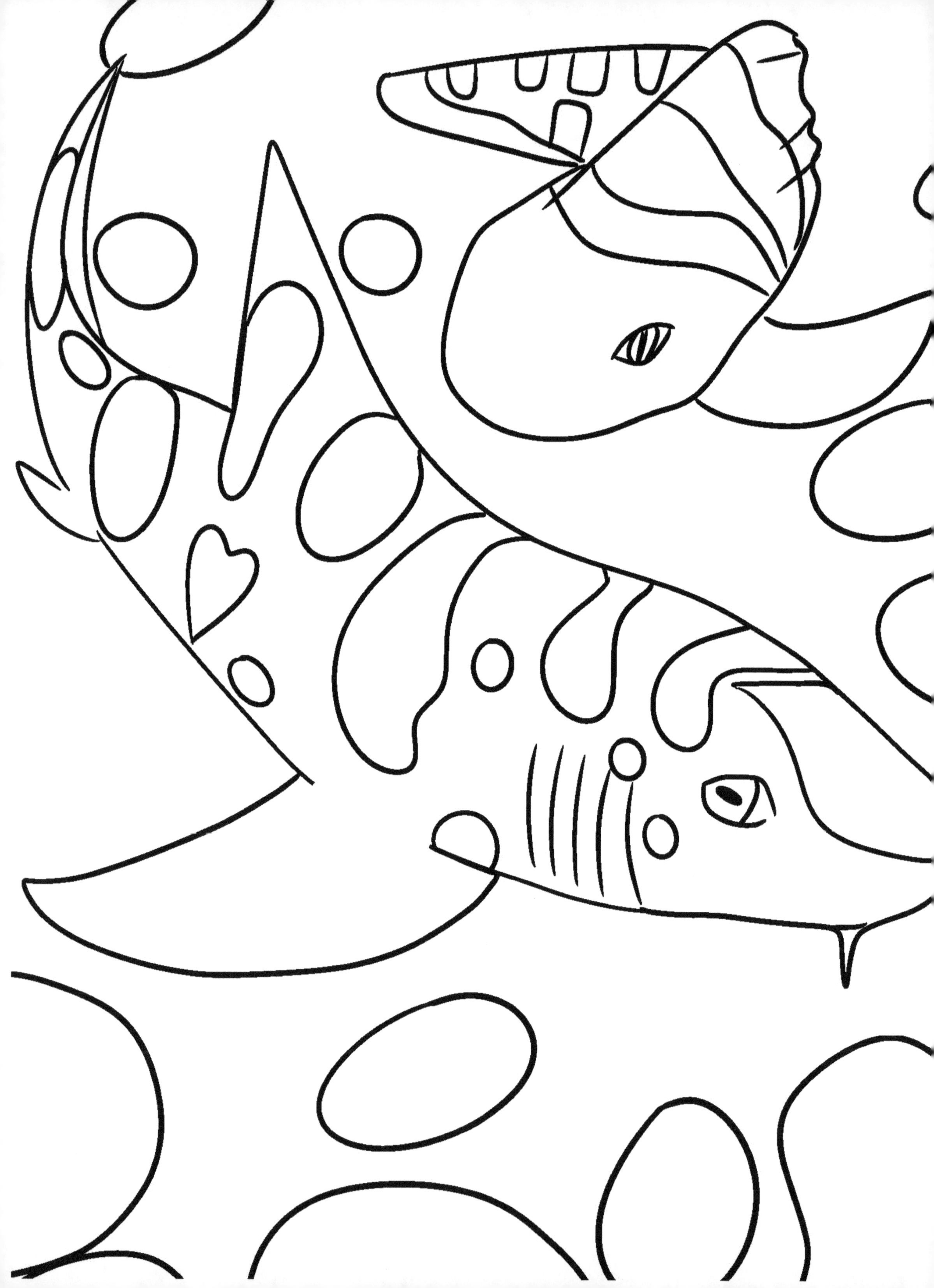

THE END!

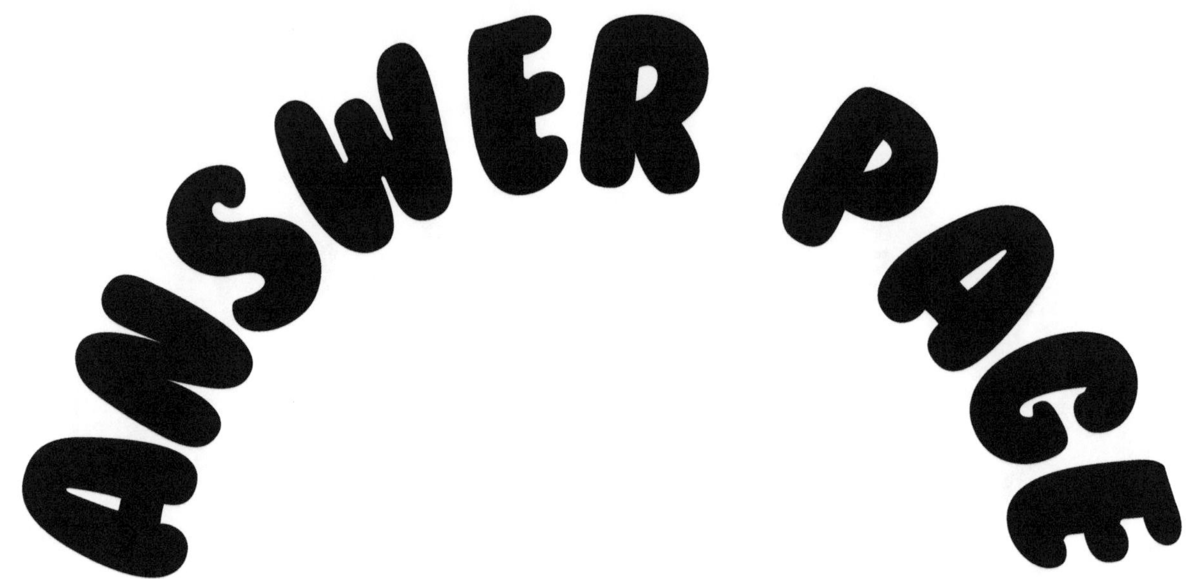

- **A chameleon is a reptile.**
- **An eel is cold blooded.**
- **A jumping spider is no blooded.**
- **A kangaroo is warm blooded.**
- **A newt is an amphibian.**
- **A pangolin is a mammal.**
- **A quail is a bird.**
- **A snail is a bug.**
- **A x-ray tetras is a fish.**